One People, One Heart

Dan & Brenda Cathcart

Cover Design: by Dan Cathcart

ISBN: 1976465818
EAN-13: 978-1976465819

Other works by Dan & Brenda Cathcart
> Shadows of the Messiah in the Torah, Vol. 1-4
> The Sign of Jonah
> Reasons for Christians to Celebrate the Biblical Feasts
> Divine Appointments with God:
> An in-depth study of the Feasts of the LORD
> Babylon Rising

Published by Moed Publishing, Auburn, WA

Visit us on the web at www.moedministries.com

One People, One Heart

Table of Contents

The pictures in this book are artistic renderings of original photographs taken by the authors at Ramat HaNadiv Gardens and Nature Preserve near Zikron Ya'akov, Israel. The gardens are dedicated to the memory of Baron Edmund Rothschild who dedicated his life and fortune to the return of the Jewish people to their ancestral homeland and the foundation of the modern State of Israel. Baron Rothschild and his wife, Adelheid are interred in a special tomb in the center of the gardens.

Introduction

2 Chronicles 30:12 NKJV Also the hand of God was on Judah to give them singleness of heart to obey the command of the king and the leaders, at the word of the LORD.

I've spent many hours pondering and meditating over this verse. After studying this situation and related situations, Dan and I wrote a twenty minute video teaching titled "Singleness of Heart" about the importance of having one heart toward God and each other. You can find this teaching at our website www.moedministries.com, by selecting our blog, and searching for "Singleness of Heart," or you can follow this link:
https://moedtorah.blogspot.com/2016/06/singleness-of-heart-hd.html

But this video teaching only included a small portion of what we had learned about having one heart. While we were in Sabbath services one day, as we rose to pray, God "downloaded" a few more places in scripture where He had demonstrated the importance of singleness of heart as well as an overall recurring theme of brotherhood. In essence, God gave me an outline for this book. I was so excited; I think I told a dozen people about this project before services were concluded!

The message of one heart is an essential one for the body of believers today as well as for national Israel. In this time when the coming of Yeshua is getting closer and closer, it is crucial for us to come together in our love for God. We may have differences in points of doctrine, but these will all be resolved at Yeshua's return. We can agree to disagree about many issues as long as we agree in our love for the God of Abraham, Isaac, and Jacob and in our belief in the coming of Messiah. As a follower of Yeshua, I believe that He is the returning Messiah although I know my Jewish friends do not. However, when we unite together in our love for God, we unleash the power of God! I believe this will happen for the Jewish people as they someday face a concerted and unified effort from their Islamic neighbors to destroy Israel. I believe this will happen for believers around the world when they are confronted with tribulation as the empire of Antichrist comes to power.

This singleness of heart won't come without prayer and repentance. In the context of this verse in 2 Chronicles, King

Hezekiah and the prophet Isaiah led the people in repentance and returning to worship God and only God! In this book, Dan and I examine the power of God that is released when we have singleness of heart toward God and each other. Won't you join me to pray that God will raise up leaders who love God with all their hearts and that He will give singleness of heart to God's people to follow these spiritual leaders at the word of the LORD?

King Hezekiah and King Josiah

2 Chronicles 30:12 NKJV 12 Also the hand of God was on Judah to give them singleness of heart to obey the command of the king and the leaders, at the word of the LORD.

The power of God that is released when God's people have singleness of heart is dramatically demonstrated when we compare the historical events at the time of King Hezekiah and King Josiah. These two kings both loved God with all their hearts and sought to restore the worship of God after a period of idolatry. Both kings restored the temple and temple worship. Both kings destroyed the altars to other gods that had been erected in Judah. Yet, the outcomes of the reigns of these two kings were vastly different. Let's look at the historical context and the particular situations of both of these kings.

After the reign of King Solomon, his son Rehoboam became king of Israel. Rehoboam instituted harsh taxes of both monetary and required servitude. Ten of the tribes of Israel rejected his authority over them and chose Jeroboam to be their king. Only the tribe of Benjamin stayed faithful to Rehoboam and the house of David from the tribe of Judah. The ten tribes who rejected Rehoboam all had their tribal lands in the north; this became the northern kingdom of Israel. Those who remained with Rehoboam formed the reduced in size southern kingdom of Judah.

The two kingdoms that were once united continually feuded back and forth. Although there were periods of alliance and reduced hostility, the relationship between the two kingdoms was generally tense and antagonistic.

King Hezekiah came to reign at a time of turmoil as the Assyrian Empire began to flex its muscles and extend its borders south towards Egypt. The northern kingdom of Israel had already been taken over as a vassal state to Assyria and the very existence of the nation of Judah was threatened.

The whole situation was set up by a war between the northern kingdom of Israel and Judah during the reign of Hezekiah's father, King Ahaz. The kingdom of Syria, located to the east of Israel, was allied with Israel against Judah. Judah was losing badly; so badly that King Ahaz set up altars to the gods of Syria thinking that the gods of Syria were more powerful than the God of Judah and Israel.

2 Chronicles 28:22-23 NKJV 22 Now in the time of his distress King Ahaz became increasingly unfaithful to the LORD. This is that King Ahaz. 23 For he sacrificed to the gods of Damascus which had defeated him, saying, "Because the gods of the kings of Syria help them, I will sacrifice to them that they may help me." But they were the ruin of him and of all Israel.

King Ahaz hedged his bets, though, by sending gifts of tribute to King Tiglath-Pileser of Assyria and asking for help against Syria and Israel. King Ahaz continued to pay tribute to Assyria for the remainder of his reign. King Tiglath-Pileser did come against both Syria and Israel, but exacted heavy tribute from King Ahaz for doing so. King Tiglath-Pileser conquered Syria and took the northeast region of the land of Israel. His successor, King Shalmanezer, eventually conquered Israel and took the people captive. But four years before Shalmenezer besieged and conquered Israel, Ahaz died and Hezekiah came to power in Judah.

2 Kings 18:9-10 NKJV 9 Now it came to pass in the fourth year of King Hezekiah, which was the seventh year of Hoshea the son of Elah, king of Israel, that Shalmaneser king of Assyria came up against Samaria and besieged it. 10 And at the end of three years they took it. In the sixth year of Hezekiah, that is, the ninth year of Hoshea king of Israel, Samaria was taken.

With the defeat of the northern kingdom of Israel, things were not looking good for the tiny nation of Judah. Assyria had gobbled up all the nations around Judah not just Israel and Syria. There was no buffer between Judah and the mighty Assyrian Empire. The Assyrian Empire was now a threat to the kingdom of Judah. But when Hezekiah came to power, he didn't let anything stop him. He immediately restored the worship of God. He opened the doors of the temple and removed the altars and high places throughout Judah.

2 Chronicles 29:3 NKJV 3 In the first year of his reign, in the first month, he opened the doors of the house of the LORD and repaired them.

Because of His trust in the LORD, the LORD blessed Judah.

2 Kings 18:7-8 NKJV 7 The LORD was with him; he prospered wherever he went. And he rebelled against the king of Assyria and did not serve him. 8 He subdued the Philistines, as far as Gaza and its territory, from watchtower to fortified city.

While Shalmanezer was busy with resettling the people of the northern kingdom of Israel in other areas of the Assyrian Empire, Hezekiah was strengthening Judah and subduing her enemies to the south. Hezekiah cut off the tribute that his father had been paying to Assyria. From a human point of view, this looked like a disastrous decision! Eight years after the fall of Israel, Assyria, now under King Sennacherib and determined to punish Judah for her rebellion, began its campaign against Judah.

2 Kings 18:13 NKJV 13 And in the fourteenth year of King Hezekiah, Sennacherib king of Assyria came up against all the fortified cities of Judah and took them.

It looked like Judah would fall just like Israel fell. The army of Assyria was both massive and well trained. They quickly conquered the outlying cities of Judah and surrounded Jerusalem with an army of 185,000 soldiers. Who could possibly save tiny Judah? But God had been working in the lives of His people in Judah! Hezekiah was a very different king than his father Ahaz.

After Hezekiah opened the doors of the temple on the first day of the first month of his reign, he restored the priesthood, the service of the Levites, and the articles of the temple. He, then, rededicated the temple to the LORD starting on the eighth day of the first month and completing it on the sixteenth day.

2 Chronicles 29:20-21 NKJV 20 Then King Hezekiah rose early, gathered the rulers of the city, and went up to the house of the LORD. 21 And they brought seven bulls, seven rams, seven lambs, and seven male goats for a sin offering for the kingdom, for the sanctuary, and for Judah. Then he commanded the priests, the sons of Aaron, to offer them on the altar of the LORD.

As Hezekiah set up for the rededication ceremony, God was working behind the scenes preparing the people. The result of this preparation was a people ready to worship God.

2 Chronicles 29:36 NKJV 36 Then Hezekiah and all the people rejoiced that God had prepared the people, since the events took place so suddenly.

These events all took place within a sixteen-day period of time! At the beginning of this interval, Judah had been worshiping the gods of Syria. The temple of the LORD was closed and left to fall to ruin. All of sudden, King Hezekiah came to power and the very first thing he did on the first day of his reign was to open the temple of the LORD! Within eight days, the temple was repaired and the rededication was set to begin. How could a people who had been worshiping other gods possibly understand this abrupt change of gods and be ready to worship the true God? The only way is that God had prepared the people ahead of time!

Since God had prepared the people, this dedication ceremony was a time of true worship. The chronicler mentions repeatedly that the people worshiped! First, we read that the gathered assembly of people bowed and worshiped. Then, we read that the king and his advisors bowed and worshiped. Finally, we read that the priests bowed and worshiped!

2 Chronicles 29:28-30 NKJV 28 So all the assembly worshiped, the singers sang, and the trumpeters sounded; all this continued until the burnt offering was finished. 29 And when they had finished offering, the king and all who were present with him bowed and worshiped. 30 Moreover King Hezekiah and the leaders commanded the Levites to sing praise to the

LORD with the words of David and of Asaph the seer. So they sang praises with gladness, and they bowed their heads and worshiped.

The scripture records that all three of the divisions of the people of Israel bowed and worshiped! Their hearts were truly prepared by God!

After the rededication ceremony, Hezekiah sent out invitations to all Judah and Israel, to come up to Jerusalem to celebrate the Passover of the LORD! Hezekiah even invited the people from the northern ten tribes to join in the celebration of Passover. Since they had missed the time of Passover in the first month, Hezekiah determined to celebrate it in the second month.

2 Chronicles 30:1 NKJV 1 And Hezekiah sent to all Israel and Judah, and also wrote letters to Ephraim and Manasseh, that they should come to the house of the LORD at Jerusalem, to keep the Passover to the LORD God of Israel.

He urged the people of Israel and Judah to repent and turn back to their God! Many of the residents of Israel received the invitation with mocking but others received it with joy and went up to Jerusalem to worship the LORD. It was as the people went up to Jerusalem for Passover that God gave the people singleness of heart!

2 Chronicles 30:12 NKJV 12 Also the hand of God was on Judah to give them singleness of heart to obey the command of the king and the leaders, at the word of the LORD.

So, when Sennacherib attacked Judah fourteen years later, the people of Judah were following their king and leaders who in turn were following God. At first Hezekiah tried to buy off Sennacherib, but that didn't work. So, Hezekiah prepared the city. He built his famous tunnel to bring water into the city from the spring of Gihon to the pool of Siloam. He built up the walls and prepared the city. Then Sennacherib sent a letter to Hezekiah demanding his unconditional surrender. Hezekiah took the letter to the temple before the LORD and asked God to save Judah for the glory of God.

2 Kings 19:19 NKJV 19 "Now therefore, O LORD our God, I pray, save us from his hand, that all the kingdoms of the earth may know that You are the LORD God, You alone."

Hezekiah had the weight of all the people behind him. They had singleness of heart to follow their king. As a result of Hezekiah's prayer, God destroyed the Assyrian army. Although King Hezekiah had prepared his army, they had nothing to do with defeating the Assyrian army. It was totally and unquestionably a direct act of God!

2 Kings 19:35-36 NKJV 35 And it came to pass on a certain night that the angel of the LORD went out, and killed in the camp of the Assyrians one hundred and eighty-five thousand; and when people arose early in the morning, there were the corpses-all dead. 36 So Sennacherib king of Assyria departed and went away, returned home, and remained at Nineveh.

Mighty Assyria never did conquer tiny Judah. Judah remained an independent nation surrounded on all sides by the Assyrian Empire! Judah's singleness of heart and King Hezekiah's prayer led to their protection and the destruction of the Assyrian army.

Three generations later, the situation in Judah was very much the same as it was when Hezekiah became king. Hezekiah's son and grandson had once again led Judah into idolatry. Instead of closing the temple, they built altars to other gods in the temple. They rebuilt all the high places of worship throughout Israel and Judah. When Hezekiah's great-grandson Josiah became king, Josiah purged the temple, Jerusalem, Judah and all of Israel from the idols that had been erected over the centuries from the time of Solomon.

Like Hezekiah, Josiah loved the LORD with all his heart.

2 Kings 23:25 NKJV 25 Now before him there was no king like him, who turned to the LORD with all his heart, with all his soul, and with all his might, according to all the Law of Moses; nor after him did any arise like him.

The scriptures testify that he fulfilled the words of the Sh'ma commanding Israel to love God with all their heart, soul and might.

Deuteronomy 6:4-5 NKJV 4 "Hear, O Israel: The LORD our God, the LORD is one! 5 "You shall love the LORD your God with all your heart, with all your soul, and with all your strength.

This was a man that truly loved the LORD! He set the example for his people and went beyond even the actions of King Hezekiah. He renewed the covenant with God!

2 Chronicles 34:30-31 NKJV 30 The king went up to the house of the LORD, with all the men of Judah and the inhabitants of Jerusalem-the priests and the Levites, and all the people, great and small. And he read in their hearing all the words of the Book of the Covenant which had been found in the house of the LORD. 31 Then the king stood in his place and made a covenant before the LORD, to follow the LORD, and to keep His commandments and His testimonies and His statutes with all his heart and all his soul, to perform the words of the covenant that were written in this book.

Then, like Hezekiah, he invited everyone from Judah and throughout Israel, from Dan in the north to Beersheva in the south, to come and celebrate the Passover of the LORD. The scriptures tell us that there was not a Passover like this one since the time of Samuel!

2 Chronicles 35:18 NKJV 18 There had been no Passover kept in Israel like that since the days of Samuel the prophet; and none of the kings of Israel had kept such a Passover as Josiah kept, with the priests and the Levites, all Judah and Israel who were present, and the inhabitants of Jerusalem.

Josiah put away all those who practiced divination and acted as priests to other gods. He ensured that the people of Israel followed only the LORD.

2 Chronicles 34:33 NKJV 33 Thus Josiah removed all the abominations from all the country that belonged to the children of Israel, and made all who were present in Israel diligently serve the LORD their God. All his days they did not depart from following the LORD God of their fathers.

But it wasn't enough. When Pharaoh Necho came out of Egypt to go to the aid of Assyria against the rebellion of Babylon, Josiah stepped in to prevent Necho from crossing Israel on their way to the aid of Assyria. God did not act to deliver Josiah and Israel from out of the hand of Pharaoh

Necho and, ultimately, out of the hand of the victorious Babylonian army. Instead, Josiah died in battle.

2 Kings 23:29 NKJV 29 In his days Pharaoh Necho king of Egypt went to the aid of the king of Assyria, to the River Euphrates; and King Josiah went against him. And Pharaoh Necho killed him at Megiddo when he confronted him.

All the people of Israel loved Josiah and mourned at his death.

2 Chronicles 35:24b-25 NKJV 24 So he died, and was buried in one of the tombs of his fathers. And all Judah and Jerusalem mourned for Josiah. 25 Jeremiah also lamented for Josiah. And to this day all the singing men and the singing women speak of Josiah in their lamentations. They made it a custom in Israel; and indeed they are written in the Laments.

What was different in this situation? Why didn't God act to save Josiah's life so he could continue to guide Israel in following God? The difference was in the heart of the people. The Young's Literal Translation of 2 Chronicles 34:33 says that Josiah caused the people to serve the LORD and that the people didn't depart from serving the LORD while Josiah lived.

2 Chronicles 34:33 YLT 33 And Josiah turneth aside all the abominations out of all the lands that the sons of Israel have, and causeth every one who is found in Israel to serve, to serve Jehovah their God; all his days they turned not aside from after Jehovah, God of their fathers.

The people followed Josiah because they loved Josiah, not because they loved God. The whole land mourned when he died; songs of mourning were written about Josiah in the Laments. The people only followed God as long as Josiah lived! The prophet Jeremiah prophesied during Josiah's reign and was one who mourned Josiah. He also spoke judgment against Judah for not turning to the LORD with all their heart!

Jeremiah 3:10 NKJV 10 "And yet for all this her treacherous sister Judah has not turned to Me with her whole heart, but in pretense," says the LORD.

At the time of Josiah, the people of Judah did not have singleness of heart toward God. They cooperated with Josiah in removing the idols from the land but they didn't remove them from their hearts. They worshiped and served God because Josiah caused them to do so, not because they loved God! Remember, when the scriptures describe the dedication of the temple of God during the reign of King Hezekiah, there are three references to the people specifically worshiping God. In fact, the people are the first ones mentioned as bowing and worshiping God!

The pretense of serving God during Josiah's reign ends with Josiah's death. As soon as Josiah died, they turned back to their idols that Josiah's father, Amon, and grandfather, Manasseh, led them to worship. The habit of their idol worship at the time of Josiah's grandfather and father was too great to overcome and judgment on Judah was inevitable.

2 Kings 24:3-4 NKJV 3 Surely at the commandment of the LORD this came upon Judah, to remove them from His sight because of the sins of Manasseh, according to all that he had done, 4 and also because of the innocent blood that he had shed; for he had filled Jerusalem with innocent blood, which the LORD would not pardon.

As a result of this blatant idolatry, Judah was conquered and taken into exile.

Within three months of Josiah's death, Pharaoh Necho, on his way back to Egypt from the defeat of the Assyrian army at Carchemish, plunders Jerusalem and takes the new king, Jehoahaz captive. Judah was required to pay tribute to Egypt. Then eight years later, Babylon demanded that Judah pay tribute to them. The cycle leading to captivity and exile had begun. Within twenty years of Josiah's death, Judah had fallen to Babylon and all her princes were taken captive.

Both Hezekiah and Josiah loved God and led the people of Judah and even the northern tribes remaining in Israel back to the worship of the one true God. The outcomes of the battles they faced were vastly different because of the difference in the hearts of the people. Under Hezekiah, God gave the people singleness of heart to follow their leaders who in turn followed God. This released the power of God when the Assyrians came up to conquer the land.

It doesn't take much imagination to realize that the tiny nation of Israel is currently in a situation almost identical to that which they faced at the time of King Hezekiah. Now is a good time to pray that God will give the people of Israel singleness of heart to follow their leaders and that their leaders will follow God.

Discussion Questions:

1. King Josiah's faith acted as a covering for the people of Judah. While he reigned, Judah was blessed. Paul talks about the importance of covering in 1 Corinthians 7:13-14. How can we be a covering for the various people in our lives?

2. What role does worship have in releasing the power of God?

I Will Take You Out to Bring You In

Exodus 19:8 NKJV Then all the people answered together and said, "All that the LORD has spoken we will do." So Moses brought back the words of the people to the LORD.

When the children of Israel arrived at Mt. Sinai, they had faced the challenges of pharaoh at the Red Sea, the bitter water at Mara, and the lack of food and water resulting in God providing manna from heaven and water from the rock. As they arrived at Mt. Sinai, they had unity of heart. It is here, at this time and place, that God offered them the covenant and the people accepted it in one accord.

The Hebrew word that is translated as "together" is "yachad," #3162 in the Strong's Concordance, which means unity. The children of Israel answered in unity. They were of one heart! Six days later, when God appeared on the mountain with great thunderings and lightnings, all the people were gathered together at the base of the mountain to hear God's voice. The word "thunderings" is the Hebrew word "kohl" #6963 in the Strong's Concordance meaning voice. In this case it is in the plural; there were voices! The Hebrew word for "lightnings" is "barraq" #1300 meaning lightning from a word meaning to lighten, glitter or flash. The Jewish sages say that God's voice was in the thunderings speaking in all the voices or languages of man, and that the lightnings were flashes or tongues of flame touching the head of each person gathered at the base of the mountain. Each person present entered into the covenant there at Mt. Sinai as God spoke these words:

Exodus 20:1-2 NKJV 1 And God spoke all these words, saying: 2 "I am the LORD your God, who brought you out of the land of Egypt, out of the house of bondage.

The Jewish sages say that if the children of Israel had stayed in unity of heart with God, they would have brought about the coming of the Messiah at that time. They would certainly have been able to release the power of God to decisively take the Promised Land. But the children of Israel did not maintain unity with each other or with God for very long. After only forty days, they turned away from God and built and worshiped the golden calf. Then, when they arrived at the entrance to the Promised Land, they turned away and refused to go into the land. Instead of releasing the power of

God to conquer the land, they doubted God and were convinced He meant to kill them!

Numbers 14:3 NKJV 3 "Why has the LORD brought us to this land to fall by the sword, that our wives and children should become victims? Would it not be better for us to return to Egypt?"

They ended up wandering in the wilderness for forty years until all the men of that generation died. When the forty years were up, they were on the plains of Moab opposite Jericho at the entrance to the Promised Land. In the final month before crossing the Jordan River and entering the land, Moses spoke all the words recorded in the book of Deuteronomy. Moses began by reciting all that God had done for them from bringing them out of Egypt to the present time. He then changed his focus to God's instructions for them. Those instructions begin in chapter 6 with the admonition to keep God's commandments, statutes, and judgments followed by an emphatic call, "Hear, O Israel." These words are known as the "sh'ma;" it is the call to hear and obey.

Deuteronomy 6:4-5 NKJV 4 "Hear, O Israel: The LORD our God, the LORD is one! 5 "You shall love the LORD your God with all your heart, with all your soul, and with all your strength.

The word "one" in this passage is the Hebrew word "echad" #259 meaning united, one, alike, together. It does not mean one in the sense of counting one object. It means one as in coming together as one, or united as one. All aspects of God are one: Elohim, El Shaddai, El Elyon, Adonai, Yahweh, Yahweh Nissi, Yahweh Raah, Yahweh Rapha, Yahweh Shammah, Yahweh Tsidkenu, Yahweh Mekoddishkem, El Olam, Yahweh Jireh, Yahweh Shalom, Yahweh Tzabaoth. He is one God. The word echad is the same word translated as "singleness" in 2 Chronicles 30:12 when God gave Judah singleness of heart.

As we see in verse five in this passage, the imperative is to love with the entirety of the heart, soul, and strength. This is singleness of heart!

As we continue in this passage, Moses first explains the blessings of God and then warns against idolatry, against loving other gods! The blessings of obedience are explained in Deuteronomy 7:12-16. They include having many children and abundance of crops and livestock. No man or woman would be barren; there would be no sickness of either the people or the livestock. They would have power over all the people who were currently in the land to drive them out. Moses reiterates the blessings and expands on them in chapter 28. He concludes that the results of loving God with all their hearts resulting in obedience would be that He would establish them as His special people.

Deuteronomy 28:9-10 NKJV 9 "The LORD will establish you as a holy people to Himself, just as He has sworn to you, if you keep the commandments of the

LORD your God and walk in His ways. 10 "Then all peoples of the earth shall see that you are called by the name of the LORD, and they shall be afraid of you.

All the nations they encountered would see the connection they have with God and be afraid!

As the children of Israel got ready to enter the land, it was time for Moses to die and for Joshua to take over. It was essential that this transition happen smoothly and that all the people know that Joshua was God's chosen leader. The scriptures describe the ceremony that inaugurated Joshua as the new leader.

Numbers 27:18-20 NKJV 18 And the LORD said to Moses: "Take Joshua the son of Nun with you, a man in whom is the Spirit, and lay your hand on him; 19 "set him before Eleazar the priest and before all the congregation, and inaugurate him in their sight. 20 "And you shall give some of your authority to him, that all the congregation of the children of Israel may be obedient.

As Joshua prepared to lead the children of Israel into the land, all the people answered Joshua with almost the same words they used at Mt. Sinai, "All that the LORD has spoken, we will do."

Joshua 1:16-18 NKJV 16 So they answered Joshua, saying, "All that you command us we will do, and wherever you send us we will go. 17 "Just as we heeded Moses in all things, so we will heed you. Only the LORD your God be with you, as He was with Moses. 18 "Whoever rebels against your command and does not heed your words, in all that you command him, shall be put to death. Only be strong and of good courage."

So, as they entered the land, they followed Joshua at the word of the LORD. Their first battle was against the city of Jericho on the Jordan River. Joshua was met by a man whom he discovered was the divine presence of God. When Joshua asked the man which side he was on, the man quickly set Joshua straight. It's not which side the man was on, but which side Joshua was on!

Joshua 5:13-15 NKJV 13 And it came to pass, when Joshua was by Jericho, that he lifted his eyes and looked, and behold, a Man stood opposite him with His sword drawn in His hand. And Joshua went to Him and said to Him, "Are You for us or for our adversaries?" 14 So He said, "No, but as Commander of the army of the LORD I have now come." And Joshua fell on his face to the earth and worshiped, and said to Him, "What does my Lord say to His servant?" 15 Then the Commander of the LORD'S army said to Joshua, "Take your sandal off your foot, for the place where you stand is holy." And Joshua did so.

This man is the captain of the army of the LORD; he is on the LORD's side. Will Joshua follow the captain of the LORD's army? Joshua responded by immediately taking off his sandals and worshipping. He was on the LORD's side and all the people followed Joshua.

As a result, God acted miraculously for the children of Israel. The wall of the city fell to trumpeting blasts of the ram's horns not to the physical blasts of battering rams! God brought down the walls!

Joshua 6:20-21 NKJV 20 So the people shouted when the priests blew the trumpets. And it happened when the people heard the sound of the trumpet, and the people shouted with a great shout, that the wall fell down flat. Then the people went up into the city, every man straight before him, and they took the city. 21 And they utterly destroyed all that was in the city, both man and woman, young and old, ox and sheep and donkey, with the edge of the sword.

The conquest of the land had begun. God had demonstrated that His presence was with them and that they could defeat any foe. But their invincibility didn't last long. Achan greedily decided to take plunder from Jericho that God had told them belonged to the treasury of the LORD. The Stone Edition Tanach translates this passage as:

Joshua 6:17-19 The city—it and all that is in it—shall be consecrated property for HASHEM. Only Rahab the innkeeper shall live—she and all who are with her in the house—because she hid the emissaries whom we sent. Only you—beware of the consecrated property, lest you cause destruction if you take from the consecrated property and you bring destruction upon the camp of Israel and cause it trouble. All the silver and gold and vessels of copper and iron are holy to HASHEM; they shall go to the treasury of the LORD.[1]

Achan's sin broke the unity of the people. They no longer had one heart toward God. Achan's heart belonged to his own selfish desires. Achan's name reflects his character; it means trouble! He stole from God and caused the defeat of the children of Israel at Ai. As a result of this sin, the Children of Israel were soundly defeated at Ai. Joshua cried out to God in despair at their defeat. God's answer explained that Israel could not stand against their enemy because of Achan's sin.

Joshua 7:10-12 ASV 10 And Jehovah said unto Joshua, Get thee up; wherefore art thou thus fallen upon thy face? 11 Israel hath sinned; yea, they have even transgressed my covenant which I commanded them: yea, they have even taken of the devoted thing, and have also stolen, and dissembled also; and they have even put it among their own stuff. 12 Therefore the children of Israel cannot stand before their enemies;

---

[1] The Stone Edition Tanach; Edited by Rabbi Noson Scherman; Mesorah Pulbications, ltd.; 2007; Page 529

they turn their backs before their enemies, because
they are become accursed: I will not be with you any
more, except ye destroy the devoted thing from among
you.

Notice that all Israel were counted as having transgressed the covenant because of the sin of the one man. There is a Hebrew word play going on in these two verses. The words translated devoted thing and accursed are from the same Hebrew word cherem #2764 in the Strong's Concordance. Cherem literally refers to something that is shut in. As such it can mean something that is devoted, dedicated, accursed, doomed or even utterly destroyed.

An item that is designated cherem is totally inaccessible to the people. Once it is designated cherem; it is out of reach! Leviticus states that anything that is cherem (devoted) to the LORD cannot be redeemed.

Leviticus 27:28 NKJV 28 'Nevertheless no devoted
offering (cherem) that a man may devote (cherem) to
the LORD of all that he has, both man and beast, or
the field of his possession, shall be sold or redeemed;
every devoted offering (cherem) is most holy to the
LORD.

Further, the book of Deuteronomy indicates that touching items that are designated cherem causes whoever touches it to be cherem. In other words cherem, like holiness, is contagious!

Deuteronomy 7:26 NKJV 26 "Nor shall you bring an abomination into your house, lest you be doomed to destruction (cherem) like it. You shall utterly detest it and utterly abhor it, for it is an accursed thing (cherem).

Achan's actions were, in fact, described as an abomination in Israel.

The Stone Edition Tanach[2] continues to explain what must happen to Achan in Joshua 7:15:

> *"It will be that the one singled out with consecrated property shall be burned, he and all that is his, because he has violated the covenant of HASHEM, and because he has committed an abomination in Israel."*

Achan took that which was to be (cherem) devoted to God and, as a result he became (cherem) accursed. The devoted thing became more than just what Achan stole; it was Achan, his family, his livestock and all his belongings. In addition, the whole state of Israel was in danger of being cherem! The Children of Israel had to destroy the (cherem) devoted thing. This is why God's judgment was especially harsh. Joshua tells us that Achan and his entire family were stoned and then burned with all their possessions.

---

[2] Ibid; page 533

Joshua 7:24-26 ASV 24 And Joshua, and all Israel with him, took Achan the son of Zerah, and the silver, and the mantle, and the wedge of gold, and his sons, and his daughters, and his oxen, and his asses, and his sheep, and his tent, and all that he had: and they brought them up unto the valley of Achor. 25 And Joshua said, Why hast thou troubled us? Jehovah shall trouble thee this day. And all Israel stoned him with stones; and they burned them with fire, and stoned them with stones. 26 And they raised over him a great heap of stones, unto this day; and Jehovah turned from the fierceness of his anger. Wherefore the name of that place was called, The valley of Achor, unto this day.

The name Achor comes from the Hebrew word "akar" #5916 in Strong's Concordance meaning to roil water, to disturb, afflict, or trouble. The place was called the valley of Trouble. This is the same root word for the name Achan! Trouble came to all Israel because of the sin of this one man. His greed stirred up the wrath of God against the Children of Israel.

After Achan was killed, the Children of Israel once more went up against Ai. This time, instead of fleeing before the men of Ai; the men of Ai fled before the army of Israel. God caused the men of Ai to fear the army of Israel, then, God brought the victory!

The account of Achan's sin was preceded by a victorious Israel. Before his sin, the Children of Israel easily conquered

Jericho. Then Achan stole from God and the Children of Israel lost the ability to stand in battle. After Achan was killed, the Children of Israel easily conquered Ai.

After the defeat of Ai, the Bible describes a renewing of the covenant at Shechem which is situated between Mt. Ebal and Mt. Gerazim. Joshua gathers all the people together to renew the covenant. He built an altar of stone on Mt. Ebal and all the people brought offerings. Half of the tribes gathered near Mt. Ebal and half gathered near Mt. Gerazim.

Joshua 8:32-35 NKJV 32 And there, in the presence of the children of Israel, he wrote on the stones a copy of the law of Moses, which he had written. 33 Then all Israel, with their elders and officers and judges, stood on either side of the ark before the priests, the Levites, who bore the ark of the covenant of the LORD, the stranger as well as he who was born among them. Half of them were in front of Mount Gerizim and half of them in front of Mount Ebal, as Moses the servant of the LORD had commanded before, that they should bless the people of Israel. 34 And afterward he read all the words of the law, the blessings and the cursings, according to all that is written in the Book of the Law. 35 There was not a word of all that Moses had commanded which Joshua did not read before all the assembly of Israel, with the women, the little ones, and the strangers who were living among them.

In the previous section, we read that King Josiah renewed the covenant with God. Yet God did not spare Josiah and Judah when Josiah went out to battle. What was different in these two covenant ceremonies? In this ceremony at Shechem under Joshua, all the people participated. They all stood in their places around the ark; they all brought offerings before the LORD. All the people participated in the ceremony as Moses had commanded Joshua to do before they crossed the Jordan.

Deuteronomy 27:11-13 NKJV 11 And Moses commanded the people on the same day, saying, 12 "These shall stand on Mount Gerizim to bless the people, when you have crossed over the Jordan: Simeon, Levi, Judah, Issachar, Joseph, and Benjamin; 13 "and these shall stand on Mount Ebal to curse: Reuben, Gad, Asher, Zebulun, Dan, and Naphtali.

Even though the sin of Achan was a solitary sin; it was contagious and all the people were at risk. So, it took all the people coming together to renew the covenant with God at Shechem. They needed to come together with singleness of heart like they did at Mt. Sinai to have God go with them and defeat their enemies before them. For all their efforts, they never managed to drive out all their enemies. Singleness of heart to love the LORD is impossible to maintain in our own strength. We need help! In our next section, we will look at the help provided by the coming of the Holy Spirit.

Discussion Questions:

1. What role do doubt and disobedience play in hindering singleness of heart towards God?

2. Brainstorm some practices that can be done individually or with a small group that help maintain unity of heart towards God.

Yeshua's Disciples

Acts 2:1 NKJV 1 When the Day of Pentecost had fully come, they were all with one accord in one place.

The Day of Pentecost is the biblical Feast of Shavuot. It is one of God's appointed feast days and the anniversary of God's appearance on Mt. Sinai as He entered into covenant with the children of Israel. We already examined the events at Mt. Sinai and how the Children of Israel were with one accord as they made a covenant with God and received God's instructions on how to live in covenant with Him. Fifteen hundred years after the events at Mt. Sinai, the Jewish people were still celebrating the Feast of Shavuot, but at this feast, something new was about to happen!

In that eventful year, Yeshua died on Passover, was placed in the tomb as the Feast of Unleavened Bread began, and rose from the dead on the Feast of Firstfruits. Yeshua's ascension was on the fortieth day after His resurrection during the time of the counting of the omer. The counting of the omer is the fifty-day count from the Feast of Firstfruits up to the next feast, the Feast of Shavuot. After Yeshua's ascension, there were ten days remaining of this count! The disciples' expectations were high; they knew a big event was coming!

Acts 1:4-5 NKJV 4 And being assembled together with them, He commanded them not to depart from Jerusalem, but to wait for the Promise of the Father, "which," He said, "you have heard from Me; 5 "for John truly baptized with water, but you shall be baptized with the Holy Spirit not many days from now."

Yeshua's disciples spent these final ten days in the temple constantly in prayer and praise. They were filled with joy as they anticipated the Promise of the Father.

Luke 24:51-53 NKJV 51 Now it came to pass, while He blessed them, that He was parted from them and carried up into heaven. 52 And they worshiped Him, and returned to Jerusalem with great joy, 53 and were continually in the temple praising and blessing God. Amen.

The anticipation of the disciples motivated them to spend as much time as they could in the temple of God! They were so excited about what God had done and what was coming that they couldn't stay away! This Feast of Shavuot would see a re-enactment of the day at the base of Mt. Sinai when God's voice spoke in all the languages of man and lightnings of God touched each person gathered there. The disciples were gathered together in one accord when the Holy Spirit dramatically made an appearance.

Acts 2:2-6 NKJV 2 And suddenly there came a sound from heaven, as of a rushing mighty wind, and it filled the whole house where they were sitting. 3 Then there appeared to them divided tongues, as of fire, and one sat upon each of them. 4 And they were all filled with the Holy Spirit and began to speak with other tongues, as the Spirit gave them utterance. 5 And there were dwelling in Jerusalem Jews, devout men, from every nation under heaven. 6 And when this sound occurred, the multitude came together, and were confused, because everyone heard them speak in his own language.

Luke describes Peter's first speech before the Jewish people. As he spoke, three thousand Jews believed that Yeshua was the Messiah and were baptized that day! But this was just the beginning! As the days passed, the people experienced fear in the presence of the believers! Many signs and miracles were displayed!

Acts 2:42-43 NKJV 42 And they continued steadfastly in the apostles' doctrine and fellowship, in the breaking of bread, and in prayers. 43 Then fear came

upon every soul, and many wonders and signs were
done through the apostles.

The believers came together and shared everything they had among themselves. Can you imagine the trust and love they had for one another to freely share all they had! God met all their needs! They were truly of one accord!

Acts 2:46-47 KJV 46 And they, continuing daily with one accord in the temple, and breaking bread from house to house, did eat their meat with gladness and singleness of heart, 47 Praising God, and having favour with all the people. And the Lord added to the church daily such as should be saved.

They had singleness of heart! The second chapter of Acts begins and ends with the statement that the believers were of one accord coming together with singleness of heart. Their unity of heart allowed the release of the power of God through the working of the Holy Spirit! This singleness of heart didn't end at this time. The apostles had the power to heal the sick, speak boldly in the temple, and stand up to intimidation from the Sanhedrin.

After Peter and John were arrested and testified before the Sanhedrin, the believers came together still in one accord and prayed.

Acts 4:23-24 NKJV 23 And being let go, they went to their own companions and reported all that the chief priests and elders had said to them. 24 So when they heard that, they raised their voice to God with one accord and said: "Lord, You are God, who made heaven and earth and the sea, and all that is in them,

They prayed that God would continue to give them boldness to proclaim the word of the LORD.

Acts 4:29-30 NKJV 29 "Now, Lord, look on their threats, and grant to Your servants that with all boldness they may speak Your word, 30 "by stretching out Your hand to heal, and that signs and wonders may be done through the name of Your holy Servant Jesus."

The power of God shook the place where the disciples were gathered together in prayer, and once again, the Holy Spirit came on them with power!

Acts 4:31 NKJV 31 And when they had prayed, the place where they were assembled together was shaken; and they were all filled with the Holy Spirit, and they spoke the word of God with boldness.

We have been told three times that the believers were all with one accord and once that they had singleness of heart. But things get even better! The very next verse tells us that the believers continued with one heart and one soul, reminding us of the words of the Sh'ma about loving God with all their heart, soul, and strength.

Acts 4:32 NKJV 32 Now the multitude of those who believed were of one heart and one soul; neither did anyone say that any of the things he possessed was his own, but they had all things in common.

This unity resulted in great power being released for the apostles to spread the word of the resurrection!

Acts 4:33 NKJV 33 And with great power the apostles gave witness to the resurrection of the Lord Jesus. And great grace was upon them all.

Twice now, we have been told that the believers shared all that they had and no one lacked anything. We read of one believer from Cyprus who sells his property and brings the entire proceeds to the apostles.

Acts 4:36-37 NKJV 36 And Joses, who was also named Barnabas by the apostles (which is translated Son of Encouragement), a Levite of the country of Cyprus, 37 having land, sold it, and brought the money and laid it at the apostles' feet.

It wasn't long, however, before the unity of the body was challenged. Like with Achan, it was just one man. Ananias and his wife Saphira sold some property and lied about what portion they were giving to the apostles for the benefit of the body. Peter confronted them about their actions.

Acts 5:3-5 NKJV 3 But Peter said, "Ananias, why has Satan filled your heart to lie to the Holy Spirit and keep back part of the price of the land for yourself? 4 "While it remained, was it not your own? And after it was sold, was it not in your own control? Why have you conceived this thing in your heart? You have not lied to men but to God." 5 Then Ananias, hearing these words, fell down and breathed his last. So great fear came upon all those who heard these things.

Sapphira, also, when asked about her actions lied about them and immediately dropped dead. This seems like an especially harsh judgment! We have all been guilty of lying or at least shading the truth at one time or another, yet we are still living! The difference in this situation is that their deceit threatened the newly formed body of believers. This account is sandwiched between two statements that the believers were in one accord! We began with the statement that they were of one heart and one soul. After the account of Ananias and Sapphira, we read once again that fear came upon the people and that the believers were of one accord.

Acts 5:11-12 NKJV 11 So great fear came upon all the church and upon all who heard these things. 12 And through the hands of the apostles many signs and wonders were done among the people. And they were all with one accord in Solomon's Porch.

The danger had been averted, unity was preserved and the power of God continued to grow. It is at this time that we read that the power of God given to the apostles was so great that even Peter's shadow falling on a sick person was enough to bring healing!

Acts 5:14-16 NKJV 14 And believers were increasingly added to the Lord, multitudes of both men and women, 15 so that they brought the sick out into the streets and laid them on beds and couches, that at least the shadow of Peter passing by might fall on some of them. 16 Also a multitude gathered from the surrounding cities to Jerusalem, bringing sick people and those who were tormented by unclean spirits, and they were all healed.

The number of believers increased daily. The apostles were highly regarded by the people, but not by the Jewish leadership. The Sadducees, who didn't believe in the resurrection of the dead, were especially enraged. Imagine the reaction of the Sadducees! They didn't believe in the resurrection of the dead, and, then, here come these men teaching the promise of the resurrection of the dead as they heal the sick and deliver those oppressed by demons!

The high priest, who was a Sadducee, had all the apostles arrested and thrown in jail. He desperately wanted to stop the spread of the gospel! But an angel released them from prison and sent them right back into the temple to keep on preaching! They didn't run away and hide; they just went on teaching!

Acts 5:19-20 NKJV 19 But at night an angel of the Lord opened the prison doors and brought them out, and said, 20 "Go, stand in the temple and speak to the people all the words of this life."

Imagine the astonishment of the high priest, the other Sadducees, and the temple guards when the people they arrested show up back in the temple as if they had never been arrested! The guards brought the apostles before the Sanhedrin where the apostles boldly stood up for the gospel, rejected the instructions of the council to cease teaching in the name of Yeshua, and went right back to the temple!

Acts 5:41-42 NKJV 41 So they departed from the presence of the council, rejoicing that they were counted worthy to suffer shame for His name. 42 And daily in the temple, and in every house, they did not cease teaching and preaching Jesus as the Christ.

This period of explosive growth in the body of believers, as well as healings and deliverances from unclean spirits, was made possible by the singleness of heart displayed by the believers! It did not mean that there were not obstacles and persecutions. Peter and John were arrested twice and the other apostles arrested with them once. In fact, persecution was coming that would scatter the growing body of believers in Yeshua throughout the Roman world. Soon, the Gentiles, with their total ignorance of God and the Torah of Moses, would begin to believe that the God of the Jews was the one true God, and that Yeshua, His son, came to bring them salvation.

Peter was given instruction by the Holy Spirit that the Gentiles also received salvation through Yeshua. Paul received the same message through the direct voice of Yeshua when He appeared to Paul while Paul was in the temple praying. This created understandable friction between the Jewish and Gentile believers. Paul pleads with the Gentiles to maintain unity with the Jews explaining that the barriers between Jew and Gentile were removed in Messiah, and that they were now one in Christ.

Despite Paul's pleas, discord between the Jewish and Gentile believers would continue to grow. By the third century C.E., this split would be complete. The Gentile believers had rejected any observance that connected them to Judaism. They changed the Sabbath to Sunday, renamed Passover to Easter, and established their own criteria for determining when to observe it. They renamed the Feast of Weeks to the Feast of Pentecost and totally ignored God's other appointed feast days.

Jewish believers were faced with the dilemma of rejecting the Torah of God or rejecting their Messiah. Most of them chose to stay with their Messiah, but in the process, they lost all connection to their Jewish heritage.

Today, there is just as much division within the Gentile body of believers. However, Jewish believers are now being encouraged to retain their identity as Jews. More and more Jewish believers are celebrating the Feasts of the LORD. Gentile believers are slowly rediscovering their own connection to the Hebraic roots of their faith learning and experiencing the richness of the whole Word of God as they participate more fully in the Sabbath and the Feasts of the LORD.

However, we will not see days like those of the early believers again until this rift between the Jewish and Gentile believers is healed. The Gentile believers must embrace each other as well as their Jewish brethren including those who do not yet know Yeshua as their Messiah. Yeshua said that the second great commandment after loving God with all the heart, soul, and mind, is to love your neighbor as yourself.

Matthew 22:37-39 NKJV 37 Jesus said to him," 'You shall love the LORD your God with all your heart, with all your soul, and with all your mind.' 38 "This is the first and great commandment. 39 "And the second is like it: 'You shall love your neighbor as yourself.'

Discussion Questions:

1. How is the sin of Ananias and Saphira like that of Achan? See Leviticus 27:28 for background on things devoted to God.

2. Luke wrote in Acts 2:43 that the fear of God came on every soul in the presence of the signs and wonders that the apostles demonstrated. In Genesis 35:2-5, fear came on the cities that Jacob and his family passed through on their way to Bethel. How do both of these situations demonstrate the power of God when there is unity of heart towards God?

Brothers Dwelling Together in Unity

A Psalm of David

**Psalms 133:1 NKJV 1 <<A Song of Ascents. Of David.>>
Behold, how good and how pleasant it is For brethren to
dwell together in unity!**

This Psalm was written by David who was intimately
familiar with enmity between brothers. David was the eighth
son in a family that considered him not worthy to be a part of
the family. The Jewish sages say that David's father Jesse
didn't think that David was actually his son, and this doubt
about David's parentage led to friction in the family. When
Samuel went to anoint a new king over Israel, David was not
presented to Samuel as one of Jesse's sons until Samuel
asked if there was another son.

1 Samuel 16:10-11 NKJV 10 Thus Jesse made seven of his sons pass before Samuel. And Samuel said to Jesse, "The LORD has not chosen these." 11 And Samuel said to Jesse, "Are all the young men here?" Then he said, "There remains yet the youngest, and there he is, keeping the sheep." And Samuel said to Jesse, "Send and bring him. For we will not sit down till he comes here."

But even after David was anointed by Samuel, David's brothers treated him as inferior. When David's three oldest brothers joined Saul's army to fight against the Philistines, David was relegated to taking care of the sheep. David's father Jesse sent David to check on his brothers and the progress of the war. When David inquired about what prize was being offered to the one who would defeat the Philistine champion, David's oldest brother answered scornfully.

1 Samuel 17:28-29 NKJV 28 Now Eliab his oldest brother heard when he spoke to the men; and Eliab's anger was aroused against David, and he said, "Why did you come down here? And with whom have you left those few sheep in the wilderness? I know your pride and the insolence of your heart, for you have come down to see the battle." 29 And David said, "What have I done now? Is there not a cause?"

Eliab accused David of pride and insolence. This is the same attitude that Joseph's brothers have towards Joseph, that Cain has towards Abel, Ishmael has towards Isaac, and that

Esau has towards Jacob. In each case, the accusation is unjust and is instead a reflection of the character of the one making the accusation. It is not David who is prideful and insolent; it is Eliab! This is, in one sense, the story of the Bible. It is the story of man's hatred and jealousy of his brother bringing about separation between brothers and separation from God. It is only when we put aside our enmity that we can approach God. Yeshua said that anyone who, when bringing an offering, harbored hatred in his heart against his brother, must first reconcile with his brother before bringing his offering.

Matthew 5:23-24 NKJV 23 "Therefore if you bring your gift to the altar, and there remember that your brother has something against you, 24 "leave your gift there before the altar, and go your way. First be reconciled to your brother, and then come and offer your gift.

We learn that Eliab's interpretation of David's actions as prideful and insolent are unfounded. David had great faith that God would raise up a champion who could defeat Goliath the Philistine champion! It was not pride in himself that gave David the assurance to speak; it was faith in God! When no one from Israel would go against Goliath, David boldly stepped up relying not on his own strength but God's strength.

1 Samuel 17:36-37 NKJV 36 "Your servant has killed both lion and bear; and this uncircumcised Philistine will be like one of them, seeing he has defied the armies of the living God." 37 Moreover David said, "The LORD, who delivered me from the paw of the lion and from the paw of the bear, He will deliver me from the hand of this Philistine." And Saul said to David, "Go, and the LORD be with you!"

Eliab's reaction to David revealed his jealousy and hatred of David. But God gave David a friend who was closer to him than any brother. When David was brought before King Saul to honor him for defeating Goliath, Jonathan was present. God knit together the souls of David and Jonathan.

1 Samuel 18:1-4 NKJV 1 Now when he had finished speaking to Saul, the soul of Jonathan was knit to the soul of David, and Jonathan loved him as his own soul. 2 Saul took him that day, and would not let him go home to his father's house anymore. 3 Then Jonathan and David made a covenant, because he loved him as his own soul. 4 And Jonathan took off the robe that was on him and gave it to David, with his armor, even to his sword and his bow and his belt.

This is an amazing relationship. Jonathan was King Saul's heir. He should have been king after Saul, but God took the throne away from Saul and gave it to David. Jonathan should have hated David for taking his birthright, but instead Jonathan loved David. When Saul recognized that God was with David to make him king in his place, Saul tried multiple times to kill David or have him killed. But still Jonathan didn't turn away from David. Instead Jonathan makes a covenant with David!

1 Samuel 20:13b-17 NKJV 13b But if it pleases my father to do you evil, then I will report it to you and send you away, that you may go in safety. And the LORD be with you as He has been with my father. 14 "And you shall not only show me the kindness of the LORD while I still live, that I may not die; 15 "but you shall not cut off your kindness from my house forever, no, not when the LORD has cut off every one of the enemies of David from the face of the earth." 16 So Jonathan made a covenant with the house of David, saying, "Let the LORD require it at the hand of David's enemies." 17 Now Jonathan again caused David to vow, because he loved him; for he loved him as he loved his own soul.

How do you think you would react to someone virtually adopted into your family who would receive your birthright and your inheritance? Jonathan was killed in battle at the same time as Saul, so we never see how that situation would have resolved itself. But by knitting together the souls of David and Jonathan, it is almost as if both David and Jonathan inherited the kingship. When the kingdom was eventually torn away from the house of David, the tribe of Benjamin, Jonathan's tribe, remained loyal to the house of David. David and Jonathan were true brothers of one heart and one soul!

But even after the death of Saul, David is still embroiled in a brotherly conflict; this time on a tribal scale. When David was first accepted as king, it was only by his own tribe of Judah.

2 Samuel 2:1 NKJV 1, 4a It happened after this that David inquired of the LORD, saying, "Shall I go up to any of the cities of Judah?" And the LORD said to him, "Go up." David said, "Where shall I go up?" And He said, "To Hebron."... 4a Then the men of Judah came, and there they anointed David king over the house of Judah.

The other tribes of Israel rejected David as king even though they knew that Samuel had anointed David as the next king. They instead accepted Saul's son Ishboseth as king over Israel. There was war between the followers of David and the followers of Ishboseth for seven and a half years. This war was prosecuted zealously on the part of Ishboseth of the house of Saul from the tribe of Benjamin. But David did not want to fight against the house of Saul. He was a reluctant fighter and sought to make peace. Instead leaders under David and Ishboseth conspired together leading to the ultimate assassination of Ishboseth. It was not until Ishboseth was killed that David was finally accepted as king over all Israel. The words of the leaders of the other tribes of Israel when they accepted David, confirm that they knew that David was God's chosen leader all along.

2 Samuel 5:1-3 NKJV 1 Then all the tribes of Israel came to David at Hebron and spoke, saying, "Indeed we are your bone and your flesh. 2 "Also, in time past, when Saul was king over us, you were the one who led Israel out and brought them in; and the LORD said to you, 'You shall shepherd My people Israel, and be ruler over Israel.'" 3 Therefore all the elders of Israel came to the king at Hebron, and King David made a covenant with them at Hebron before the LORD. And they anointed David king over Israel.

The war between the house of David and the house of Saul that had divided all Israel was finally over. The sages say that David wrote this Psalm in honor of the uniting of all twelve tribes under the leadership of David. Josephus writes about the celebration when David was crowned King over all Israel in his book The Antiquities of the Jews, Book 7; Chapter 2, line 60:

"This multitude came together to Hebron to David, with a great quantity of corn and wine, and all other sorts of food, and established David in his kingdom with **one consent**; and when the people had rejoiced for three days in Hebron, David and all the people removed to Jerusalem."

All Israel was united as one under the kingship of David and the whole nation flourished. They were all with one accord and, thus, the nation quickly took the city of Jerusalem, which had held off the forces of Israel since the days of

Joshua and Caleb! David then went out and defeated the Philistines which had plagued the Israelites since the days of Eli the priest who judged Israel before Samuel. The nation of Israel was united in a way that it hadn't been since the time of Joshua!

David had his faults. He faltered many times and suffered the consequences of his sins. But, in every case, David repented and turned back to God. God characterized David as a man after His own heart through Samuel's words to Saul.

1 Samuel 13:14 NKJV 14 "But now your kingdom shall not continue. The LORD has sought for Himself a man after His own heart, and the LORD has commanded him to be commander over His people, because you have not kept what the LORD commanded you."

The kingdom remained united under David and the early reign of Solomon, but Solomon did not have singleness of heart towards God. He followed after the gods of his foreign wives and concubines! So, God tore the kingdom away from him leaving only Judah and Benjamin to follow the house of David. Remember that covenant between David and Jonathan! David was from the tribe of Judah and Jonathan was from the tribe of Benjamin. Benjamin remained loyal to the house of David. The rift between the tribes of Judah and Benjamin and the rest of the tribes of Israel continues to this day.

1 Kings 12:19-20 NKJV 19 So Israel has been in rebellion against the house of David to this day. 20 Now it came to pass when all Israel heard that Jeroboam had come back, they sent for him and called him to the congregation, and made him king over all Israel. There was none who followed the house of David, but the tribe of Judah only.

At the time of the split between the tribes, God intervened, preventing immediate war between the two factions, one led by Jeroboam of the tribe of Ephraim and the other led by Rehoboam of the tribe of Judah.

1 Kings 12:23-24 NKJV 23 "Speak to Rehoboam the son of Solomon, king of Judah, to all the house of Judah and Benjamin, and to the rest of the people, saying, 24 'Thus says the LORD: "You shall not go up nor fight against your brethren the children of Israel. Let every man return to his house, for this thing is from Me."'" Therefore they obeyed the word of the LORD, and turned back, according to the word of the LORD.

Although war was prevented at the time of the division of Israel, war soon erupted and continued almost without break until the northern kingdom was carried off into captivity by Assyria. This northern kingdom was often referred to as Ephraim because its first ruler, Jeroboam, was from the tribe of Ephraim. We will follow this rift between the house of David and the rest of Israel when we examine the reuniting of Ephraim and Judah.

Discussion Questions:

1. What attitude is the prevailing one between David and Jonathan? How can this guide the way we treat each other?

2. What was Rehoboam's attitude towards the children of Israel? What was their attitude toward Rehoboam (1 Kings 12)? How can this guide the way we treat each other?

Brothers in Scripture

David's strained relationship with his brothers is a common theme in scripture. It goes back to the very beginning, to the time of Adam and Eve, with Cain's jealously and hatred of Abel. It continues after the flood and the calling of Abraham with enmity between Abraham's sons Ishmael and Isaac. It continues through two more generations with enmity between Esau and Jacob and, finally, with enmity between Joseph and Judah. The enmity was halted in this generation when Judah expressed remorse and Joseph forgave Judah and his other brothers.

Genesis 45:5 NKJV 5 "But now, do not therefore be grieved or angry with yourselves because you sold me here; for God sent me before you to preserve life.

Joseph embraced his brothers and kissed them, rejoicing in being reunited with them.

Genesis 45:15 NKJV 15 Moreover he kissed all his brothers and wept over them, and after that his brothers talked with him.

This resulted in a time of prosperity and growth in the land of Egypt. Joseph provided for his entire family from his position in Egypt as second only to Pharaoh.

Genesis 47:27 NKJV 27 So Israel dwelt in the land of Egypt, in the country of Goshen; and they had possessions there and grew and multiplied exceedingly.

Although the enmity between brothers was halted in Joseph's generation, it kept popping up. In fact, it still keeps popping up! It popped up between Moses and Aaron. It popped up between different tribes as related in the book of Judges. It popped up between David's sons. Then it reemerged between the descendants of Joseph and Judah.

Many of you have experienced enmity between brothers or even sisters in your own families. God desires this enmity to be resolved through repentance, forgiveness, and mercy. However, when repentance is not present, this enmity will never completely go away until it is resolved in the Day of Judgment. When John receives the vision from Yeshua about His return, he sees the souls of the righteous who were killed for their testimony about God.

Revelation 6:9-10 NKJV 9 When He opened the fifth seal, I saw under the altar the souls of those who had been slain for the word of God and for the testimony which they held. 10 And they cried with a loud voice, saying, "How long, O Lord, holy and true, until You judge and avenge our blood on those who dwell on the earth?"

The righteous are waiting for God to judge and avenge their blood. This dates back to the first murder when Cain killed Abel. Abel was a righteous man who brought the best that he had to offer to God. Cain had the appearance of righteousness; he also brought on offering to God. But Cain's offering was not the best; it was what he had to spare. It was from the work of his hands, but it was not the best nor was it the firstfruits.

Genesis 4:3-5 NKJV 3 And in the process of time it came to pass that Cain brought an offering of the fruit of the ground to the LORD. 4 Abel also brought of the firstborn of his flock and of their fat. And the LORD respected Abel and his offering, 5 but He did not respect Cain and his offering. And Cain was very angry, and his countenance fell.

Cain was angry that God had not accepted his offering and took it out on Abel. Cain killed Abel and tried to conceal it from God. But the scripture speaks of two witnesses against Cain—Abel's blood and the earth that opened its mouth and swallowed the blood.

Genesis 4:10-11 NKJV 10 And He said, "What have you done? The voice of your brother's blood cries out to Me from the ground. 11 "So now you are cursed from the earth, which has opened its mouth to receive your brother's blood from your hand.

The earth and Abel's blood are eternal witnesses against Cain. Both cry out for vengeance to the avenger of blood. But who is the avenger of blood? What do the scriptures tell us about the role of the avenger of blood? What about the words in the book of Hebrews that tells us that Yeshua's blood speaks a better word than that of Abel's?

Hebrews 12:22-24 NKJV 22 But you have come to Mount Zion and to the city of the living God, the heavenly Jerusalem, to an innumerable company of angels, 23 to the general assembly and church of the firstborn who are registered in heaven, to God the Judge of all, to the spirits of just men made perfect, 24 to Jesus the Mediator of the new covenant, and to the blood of sprinkling that speaks better things than that of Abel.

The context of this passage is an admonition not to follow the path of Esau or those who rebelled in the wilderness. As terrible as their judgment was, it will be much worse for those who have come to Mount Zion and the salvation offered through Yeshua and then turned away.

Hebrews 12:25 NKJV 25 See that you do not refuse Him who speaks. For if they did not escape who refused Him who spoke on earth, much more shall we not escape if we turn away from Him who speaks from heaven,

Who is He that both saves and avenges? How is it possible that He can do both? To answer this, we must look at what the Bible tells us about the consequences for killing another person and the role of the avenger of blood.

After the flood, God told Noah that every man is accountable to God and, from that time forward, anyone who killed someone would have his life taken as well. God counted blood as the symbol of that life.

Genesis 9:4-6 NKJV 4 "But you shall not eat flesh with its life, that is, its blood. 5 "Surely for your lifeblood I will demand a reckoning; from the hand of every beast I will require it, and from the hand of man. From the hand of every man's brother I will require the life of man. 6 "Whoever sheds man's blood, By man his blood shall be shed; For in the image of God He made man.

God didn't make exception for the accidental taking of a life. Everyone is accountable for his deeds. But God is a just God and forgiveness is possible for the accidental taking of a life. God told Israel to set up cities of refuge for those people who accidentally killed another person. If the person who accidentally killed another person stays within the borders of the city of refuge, the avenger of blood was forbidden from touching him.

Numbers 35:10-12 NKJV 10 "Speak to the children of Israel, and say to them: 'When you cross the Jordan into the land of Canaan, 11 'then you shall appoint *cities to be cities of refuge for you, that the manslayer who kills any person accidentally may flee there. 12 'They shall be cities of refuge for you from the **avenger**, that the manslayer may not die until he stands before the congregation in judgment.*

The word "avenger" in this passage is the Hebrew word "ga-al, #1350 meaning to redeem, to avenge, to deliver, purchase or ransom. The avenger is also the redeemer, deliverer, and ransomer! As the avenger, the ga'al would be responsible for avenging the life of a relative who had been killed. As redeemer, the ga'al is the next of kin who would be responsible for redeeming property or even the relative who has been sold into slavery. Job declares that he is confident that his redeemer, ga'al, lives.

Job 19:25 NKJV 25 For I know that my Redeemer lives, And He shall stand at last on the earth;

In the book of Ruth, the word "ga'al" is translated as "kinsman" referring to Boaz. Boaz is one of Naomi's near relatives who can redeem the property of Naomi's dead husband, Elimelech. Boaz married Ruth and through that action redeemed both the property and the line of Elimelech. The role of the ga'al is to redeem, avenge, and deliver. We understand the role of the "ga'al" in avenging the blood of one who is killed. But the one who accidentally kills someone also has a "ga'al," one who delivers him!

So, a person who kills someone flees to the city of refuge. Once there, a trial will be held to determine whether the death was accidental or intentional. If the death was intentional, the killer would be delivered to the avenger of blood and the avenger will put him to death. If the death was judged accidental, the slayer of blood will be returned to the city of refuge to remain there until the high priest dies.

Numbers 35:25 NKJV 25 'So the congregation shall deliver the manslayer from the hand of the avenger of blood, and the congregation shall return him to the city of refuge where he had fled, and he shall remain there until the death of the high priest who was anointed with the holy oil.

According to the covenant with Noah, a life is required for the taking of a life. The death of the high priest satisfies the requirement of blood in payment for shedding blood. The high priest acts in the role of "ga'al" in relation to the one who has killed someone accidentally. This explains the passage in Hebrews that the blood of Yeshua speaks a better word than that of Abel's blood. Abel's blood could only condemn; Yeshua's blood can redeem. But, just like the slayer of blood must face the avenger if he leaves the city of refuge, those who turn away from Yeshua must, also, face the judgment of Yeshua, the avenger of blood.

Cain will face Yeshua, the avenger of blood, in the Day of Judgment. Cain's blood, his life, will be required of him. The enmity between Cain and Abel will be resolved. In the case of Joseph and his brothers, however, the enmity was resolved through forgiveness. Joseph and his brothers reconciled, and they lived in peace.

Discussion Questions:

1. Peter asked Yeshua how many times he should forgive his brother. Yeshua answered with a parable in Matthew 18:21-35. Yeshua also speaks about forgiveness in Luke 17:3-4 as well as in the model prayer He gave His disciples. What are the boundaries or requirements for forgiveness between brothers?

2. How is Yeshua both the avenger of blood and the kinsman redeemer? How do we reconcile His role of avenger of blood with His teaching on forgiveness?

How Good and Pleasant

Now, we turn our attention to the words of Psalm 133 extolling the benefits of brothers living together in unity.

Psalms 133:1-3 NKJV Behold, how good and how pleasant it is For brethren to dwell together in unity! 2 It is like the precious oil upon the head, Running down on the beard, The beard of Aaron, Running down on the edge of his garments. It is like the dew of Hermon, Descending upon the mountains of Zion; For there the LORD commanded the blessing-Life forevermore.

Many commentaries including the Treasury of Scripture Knowledge and those of Matthew Poole and Thomas Scott say that David wrote this Psalm in honor of the reuniting of the tribes when he became king over all Israel. The first verse of this Psalm says that it is "good" and "pleasant." These words in English lack strength and vitality. They are so overused, they seem rather anemic to us. But what are the words David used in Hebrew? Are they similarly anemic or do they have power?

The word translated as "good" is the Hebrew word "tov", #2896. Strong's Dictionary tells us it means "good, in the widest use of the word." Its first use in scripture tells us much more than this definition however. It is first used to describe the goodness of God's creation.

Genesis 1:3-4 NKJV 3 Then God said, "Let there be light"; and there was light. 4 And God saw the light, that it was good; and God divided the light from the darkness.

The English word "good" doesn't give a powerful message, but ponder for a moment the context of its use here in creation. This is the word God uses over and over again to describe every aspect of creation. Look at the sun, the moon, and the stars. What feeling do you have when you are away from the lights of the city and gaze up at the night sky? What feeling do you experience when you stare out at the mighty ocean, or look up at the tallest mountain? What feeling do you experience when you see a herd of deer or a pod of whales? What feeling do you experience when you examine the smallest cell under a microscope? This is the goodness of God's creation. This is the power of the word "tov."

The word translated as "pleasant" is the word "naw-eem," #5273 in Strong's Concordance. It is defined as delightful or pleasant. Once again, we turn to the context of its first use to get a deeper understanding of this word. Ironically, the first use is by David when he uses it to describe the relationship between King Saul and his son Jonathan.

2 Samuel 1:23 NKJV 23 "Saul and Jonathan were beloved and pleasant (naw-eem) in their lives, And in their death they were not divided; They were swifter than eagles, They were stronger than lions.

Saul and Jonathan loved each other and each took delight in the other. Considering Saul's enmity towards David, it seems odd that David would describe the relationship between Saul and Jonathan in such a way, but when we examine the actions of David, he never harbored hatred for Saul. David clearly sees and respects the bond between Saul and Jonathan. David goes on to use a form of the same word to describe his own relationship with Jonathan.

2 Samuel 1:26 NKJV 26 I am distressed for you, my brother Jonathan; You have been very pleasant (naw-eem) to me; Your love to me was wonderful, Surpassing the love of women.

Like Saul and Jonathan, David and Jonathan loved one another and delighted in the presence and accomplishments of the other. Feel the strength and power of the relationship between Saul and Jonathan and between David and Jonathan. This is the true intensity of this word we translate as "pleasant."

Putting these two words together, it is good and pleasant for brothers to dwell together in unity. This is the way it's supposed to be! It has the goodness of creation and the joy of being with one another and taking delight in each other's accomplishments.

Discussion Questions:

1. David and Jonathan were brothers of the soul. We read in John 19:26-27 and John 21:23 that Yeshua's disciple John was closer to Yeshua than any other. How did Yeshua demonstrate that love for John? How did John demonstrate that love for Yeshua?

2. Yeshua said in John 13:34-35, that His disciples will be known by their love for one another. Paul says in Romans 13:8, that loving one another fulfills the law. How do we demonstrate our love for each other and how does that fulfill the law? How is God central to that love?

As the Anointing of Aaron and the Dew of Hermon

David goes on in Psalm 133 to compare the unity of brothers to the anointing of Aaron and the dew of Hermon. The poetical form invites a visual imagery of the anointing oil flowing over Aaron which is in turn compared to dew falling on Mount Hermon. Let's start with the literal act of Aaron's anointing.

Aaron was anointed by his brother Moses as part of the ceremony dedicating Aaron and his sons as priests. This ceremony took seven days and was conducted at the same time as the ceremony dedicating the tabernacle. The book of Exodus records this event.

Exodus 29:4-7 NKJV 4 "And Aaron and his sons you shall bring to the door of the tabernacle of meeting, and you shall wash them with water. 5 "Then you shall take the garments, put the tunic on Aaron, and the robe of the ephod, the ephod, and the breastplate, and gird him with the intricately woven band of the ephod. 6 "You shall put the turban on his head, and put the holy crown on the turban. 7 "And you shall take the anointing oil, pour it on his head, and anoint him.

Skipping down to verse 35:

Exodus 29:35 NKJV 35 "Thus you shall do to Aaron and his sons, according to all that I have commanded you. Seven days you shall consecrate them.

Once again, let's put this event in its historical perspective. When God called Moses to bring the children of Israel out of Egypt, Moses was reluctant! He worried that he wouldn't be able to speak well.

Exodus 4:10 NKJV 10 Then Moses said to the LORD, "O my Lord, I am not eloquent, neither before nor since You have spoken to Your servant; but I am slow of speech and slow of tongue."

Moses was adamant that God send someone else! But God was also adamant that He was sending Moses! However, God had already prepared someone to stand beside Moses. Moses' brother Aaron was already on his way to meet Moses! And because Moses insisted that he couldn't speak to the people, God would make Aaron Moses' spokesman.

Exodus 4:14-16 NKJV 14 So the anger of the LORD was kindled against Moses, and He said: "Is not Aaron the Levite your brother? I know that he can speak well. And look, he is also coming out to meet you. When he sees you, he will be glad in his heart. 15 "Now you shall speak to him and put the words in his mouth. And I will be with your mouth and with his mouth, and I will teach you what you shall do. 16 "So he shall be

your spokesman to the people. And he himself shall be
as a mouth for you, and you shall be to him as God.

This is the first mention of Aaron in the Bible. We are not told earlier that Moses even had a brother! First mentions in the Bible are always important. So, let's look at what this first mention of Aaron tells us. First, we are assured of his lineage; that he is actually related to Moses. Second, the relationship is defined as that of brothers. In Hebrew, the word "brother" is "ach", אח. The letters that make up this word are the aleph, א, signaling strength and the chet, ח, signaling a fence. A brother provides a strong fence of protection. In today's language, we would interpret God as saying, "Hey, Moses, your brother Aaron has your back!" This is reinforced by the statement that Aaron will be "glad in his heart" to see Moses.

This meeting of Moses and Aaron was important; it would establish the working relationship between the two brothers. Where would they meet? How would they get along? What would their relationship be? First, we know that their meeting was orchestrated by God. Their meeting was on the mountain of God, the place where God appeared to Moses in the burning bush and the place that God would lead the children of Israel to after taking them out of Egypt!

Exodus 4:27 NKJV 27 And the LORD said to Aaron, "Go into the wilderness to meet Moses." So he went and met him on the mountain of God, and kissed him.

We tend to think of this meeting as taking place close to Egypt probably just before Moses crossed into Egyptian territory. But, this place was in Midian where Moses took care of Jethro's flocks. Aaron had to travel a long way to meet Moses! We don't hear anything about Aaron's trip and the faith he exhibited to travel such a distance to meet a brother he hardly knew.

When they meet, Moses explains all that God told him and from there on, the two did everything together.

Exodus 4:28-30 NKJV 28 So Moses told Aaron all the words of the LORD who had sent him, and all the signs which He had commanded him. 29 Then Moses and Aaron went and gathered together all the elders of the children of Israel. 30 And Aaron spoke all the words which the LORD had spoken to Moses. Then he did the signs in the sight of the people.

Every time Moses addressed the children of Israel or Pharaoh, Aaron was by his side acting as his spokesman. The only time they were apart was when Moses spoke to God, although sometimes God spoke to both Moses and Aaron.

Exodus 6:13 NKJV 13 Then the LORD spoke to Moses and Aaron, and gave them a command for the children of Israel and for Pharaoh king of Egypt, to bring the children of Israel out of the land of Egypt.

Both Moses and Aaron received the command from God to deliver the message that God was taking the children of Israel out of Egypt! Moses and Aaron, also, both received the instructions for the Passover, the command to leave Egypt in the night, and the ordinance of how they were to conduct the Passover in the future!

This takes us back to Mt. Sinai where things began and where things would now change between Aaron and Moses. While Moses was on the mountain of God receiving God's instructions, Aaron was left in charge of the camp. When the people grew restless because Moses was gone so long, Aaron built the golden calf for the people to worship! When Moses came down from the mountain, he confronted Aaron.

Exodus 32:21-22 NKJV 21 And Moses said to Aaron, "What did this people do to you that you have brought so great a sin upon them?" 22 So Aaron said, "Do not let the anger of my lord become hot. You know the people, that they are set on evil.

Aaron passed off the responsibility for building and worshipping the golden calf onto the people! Moses acted decisively to cut off the pagan worship, but this time Aaron was not by his side.

Exodus 32:25-26 NKJV 25 Now when Moses saw that the people were unrestrained (for Aaron had not restrained them, to their shame among their enemies), 26 then Moses stood in the entrance of the camp, and

said, "Whoever is on the LORD'S side-come to me."
And all the sons of Levi gathered themselves together
to him.

After this incident, Moses moved the tent of meeting outside of the camp. Moses stayed outside the camp with the tent of meeting for forty days before returning to Mt. Sinai for a second forty days on the mountain with God. Aaron did not go with Moses outside the camp. Instead, Moses' aid Joshua accompanied Moses. Aaron is not mentioned again in scripture until after Moses returns from the mountain. The context of this mention is that Aaron and all the people were frightened of Moses.

Exodus 34:30 NKJV 30 So when Aaron and all the
children of Israel saw Moses, behold, the skin of his
face shone, and they were afraid to come near him.

There is a clear separation between the brothers who had been virtually inseparable! Aaron is now grouped with the rest of Israel. The scriptures, then, skip ahead to the next year when the work on the tabernacle is complete. We don't know what the relationship between Aaron and Moses was during this time. God had already chosen Aaron to be the high priest before the sin of the golden calf and those plans went forward. When the tabernacle was complete, the dedication of the tabernacle as God's dwelling place, and the inauguration of Aaron and his sons as God's priests began.

Moses anointed Aaron and his sons with oil at both the beginning and the end of the first day of the dedication ceremony. The first anointing included only oil.

Leviticus 8:10-12 NKJV 10 Also Moses took the anointing oil, and anointed the tabernacle and all that was in it, and consecrated them. 11 He sprinkled some of it on the altar seven times, anointed the altar and all its utensils, and the laver and its base, to consecrate them. 12 And he poured some of the anointing oil on Aaron's head and anointed him, to consecrate him.

Moses then brought the offerings and sacrificed them, conducting the entire service. At the end of the service, Moses once again anointed Aaron and his sons, this time the anointing included the blood from the sacrifices.

Leviticus 8:30 NKJV 30 Then Moses took some of the anointing oil and some of the blood which was on the altar, and sprinkled it on Aaron, on his garments, on his sons, and on the garments of his sons with him; and he consecrated Aaron, his garments, his sons, and the garments of his sons with him.

Aaron and his sons then spend seven days at the doors of the tabernacle as part of the dedication ceremony. On the eighth day Aaron took over the ceremony. As Aaron's first service is coming to an end, Aaron comes down from the altar and blesses the people.

Leviticus 9:22 NKJV 22 Then Aaron lifted his hand toward the people, blessed them, and came down from offering the sin offering, the burnt offering, and peace offerings.

But God's presence did not come down and consume the offerings. Aaron's blessing alone did not complete the ceremony. After Aaron blessed the people, Aaron and Moses went into the tabernacle together. This is a private meeting between God, Aaron and Moses. We can only speculate on what they did when they went into the tabernacle, but when they came out, Moses and Aaron blessed the people together!

Leviticus 9:23-24 NKJV 23 And Moses and Aaron went into the tabernacle of meeting, and came out and blessed the people. Then the glory of the LORD appeared to all the people, 24 and fire came out from before the LORD and consumed the burnt offering and the fat on the altar. When all the people saw it, they shouted and fell on their faces.

When Moses and Aaron blessed the people together, fire came out from the presence of the LORD and consumed the offerings! The literal act of Aaron's anointing, culminating in the joint blessing by Moses and Aaron, opened the way for God to dwell in the midst of His people. It opened the way for the children of Israel to approach God! The offering God consumed was the offering for the entire nation. The offering is what symbolically brings the one bringing the offering into the presence of God. When Aaron and Moses were acting together, the power of God was unleashed. God's presence exploded out of the Tabernacle and consumed the offering symbolically bringing the whole camp of Israel into the presence of God!

The poetic form of Psalm 133 adds another dimension to the relationship between Aaron and Moses. The form of the verses invites the reader to invoke the imagery of Aaron's anointing. We can see Moses standing over Aaron pouring the oil liberally onto Aaron, one brother empowering another. For Moses and Aaron, this was a special occasion. Moses had acted as the priest for Israel up until this point. Now, Moses is appointing his brother to take over.

As we put ourselves into this image, another thing we would think about would be the scent of the oil.

Exodus 30:23-25 NKJV 23 "Also take for yourself quality spices-five hundred shekels of liquid myrrh, half as much sweet-smelling cinnamon (two hundred and fifty shekels), two hundred and fifty shekels of sweet-smelling cane, 24 "five hundred shekels of cassia, according to the shekel of the sanctuary, and a hin of olive oil. 25 "And you shall make from these a holy anointing oil, an ointment compounded according to the art of the perfumer. It shall be a holy anointing oil.

It must have had a wonderful aroma!

Next, we might think of the imagery invoked by the repeated use of the word "running." We can see an abundance of oil running over Aaron's head and beard and down onto his garments. Moses wasn't miserly pouring out only a drop or two! He was applying it liberally! Oil is a symbol of God's blessings and the Holy Spirit! Moses was conferring blessings, power, and authority upon Aaron! The unity of brothers is like the abundant outpouring of God's Spirit and blessings!

This leads naturally to the dew falling on Mt. Hermon and descending on Mount Zion!

> *Psalm 133:3 It is like the dew of Hermon, Descending upon the mountains of Zion; For there the LORD commanded the blessing-Life forevermore.*

Dew is compared to God's words which nourish and refresh!

> *Deuteronomy 32:2 NKJV 2 Let my teaching drop as the rain, My speech distill as the dew, As raindrops on the tender herb, And as showers on the grass.*

The dew falls on Mt. Hermon, the highest mountain in Israel and one blessed with abundance of rain and snow. Without the moisture, the land is dry and arid; crops don't grow and there is no harvest. Most of the rainfall in Israel falls to the north, with the jet stream flowing west to east over the northern part of Israel. Imagine being in Jerusalem and looking to the north and seeing rain clouds gather. You know rain is falling on Mt. Hermon and you long for the rain to come and fall on Jerusalem. As the jet stream dips to the south, it is almost as if the clouds that have dropped rain over Mt. Hermon come and drop rain over Jerusalem. Metaphorically, the dew from Mt. Hermon falls on Mt. Zion in Jerusalem. Unity between brothers is like the desperately hoped for and long-awaited dew. When unity is present, blessings follow and life flourishes!

Zion is, of course, the place of God's throne on Earth. Zion is also the place where Yeshua would die and be resurrected so that we could have eternal life. David writes that it is the place from which God commanded the blessing of eternal life! Unity between brothers, then, is like God's word, which falls on and nourishes Zion and, as a result, brings forth eternal life! David describes unity between brothers as being as desired as the word of God which brings eternal life! Once again, the imagery is strong and powerful!

God desires unity between brothers! The nation of Israel was divided at the death of David's son Solomon. Solomon's disobedience to God led to this division. The division between the house of David and the rest of the tribes of Israel has never been fully healed. David looks forward to the time when the tribes will once again unite and proclaim a son of David as king over the entire nation.

Discussion Questions:

1. Yeshua describes those who are His brothers in parallel passages in Matthew 12:46-50, Mark 3:31-35, and Luke 8:19-21. Who are Yeshua's brothers?

2. Paul describes the gift of support from the Philippian church as having a sweet aroma in Philippians 4:15-18. How is this like the sweet aroma of the anointing oil that Moses poured on Aaron's head?

Judah and Ephraim: One Stick

Ezekiel 37:17 And draw them one to one for yourself, into one stick. And they shall become for oneness in your hand. (J. P Green Interlinear Bible)

In order to understand the significance of Judah and Ephraim coming together in one stick, we need to understand the division between them. The rift between the tribe of Judah and the tribe of Ephraim dates back to the splitting of the kingdom in the time of King Rehoboam, the son of Solomon. Although Solomon started out following God, in his later years, he turned away and led Israel into idolatry.

1 Kings 11:9-10 NKJV 9 So the LORD became angry with Solomon, because his heart had turned from the LORD God of Israel, who had appeared to him twice, 10 and had commanded him concerning this thing, that he should not go after other gods; but he did not keep what the LORD had commanded.

Solomon, also, placed a heavy tax burden on the people of Israel for his many building projects. Rehoboam promised to increase the burden that Solomon had placed on them, so ten tribes of Israel used this as an excuse to rebel against the unpopular Rehoboam and side with the popular Jeroboam of the tribe of Ephraim.

2 Chronicles 10:4 NKJV 4 "Your father made our yoke heavy; now therefore, lighten the burdensome service of your father and his heavy yoke which he put on us, and we will serve you."

The nation of Israel was divided into two nations, the northern kingdom of Israel consisting of the ten tribes given to Jeroboam, the Ephraimite, and the southern kingdom consisting of Judah and Benjamin. This division lasted until the kingdom of Israel was taken captive to Assyria. Although some of the remnant of Israel came to Jerusalem to worship after the captivity, there was no healing of the rift between the tribes. The enmity between the kingdoms was severe. There was almost constant war going on between Israel and Judah. In fact, the final blow that led to the captivity of Israel was instigated by King Ahaz of Judah. King Pekah of Israel and King Rezin of Syria joined forces against Judah and besieged the city of Jerusalem.

2 Kings 16:5 NKJV 5 Then Rezin king of Syria and Pekah the son of Remaliah, king of Israel, came up to Jerusalem to make war; and they besieged Ahaz but could not overcome him.

King Ahaz sent tribute to King Tiglath-Pileser of Assyria asking him to come to his aid.

2 Kings 16:7 NKJV 7 So Ahaz sent messengers to Tiglath-Pileser king of Assyria, saying, "I am your servant and your son. Come up and save me from the hand of the king of Syria and from the hand of the king of Israel, who rise up against me."

Tiglath-Pileser attacked and defeated Syria killing King Rezin. Several years later Assyria returned to attack Israel. They succeeded after three years and took the people of Israel into captivity.

2 Kings 17:5-6 NKJV 5 Now the king of Assyria went throughout all the land, and went up to Samaria and besieged it for three years. 6 In the ninth year of Hoshea, the king of Assyria took Samaria and carried Israel away to Assyria, and placed them in Halah and by the Habor, the River of Gozan, and in the cities of the Medes.

For the entire time of its existence, the kingdom of Israel worshiped idols and rejected God. Every king followed after the sins of its founder Jeroboam. At the mention of each new king of Israel, the Bible records that the king "did evil in the sight of the LORD; he did not depart from the sins of Jeroboam the son of Nebat, who had made Israel sin."

Although King Ahaz was the one who brought in the king of Assyria to defeat and capture Israel, Assyria was victorious because God gave Israel into the hands of the Assyrians. They were conquered and carried into captivity because of their sins.

> *2 Kings 17:21b-23 NKJV 21b Then Jeroboam drove Israel from following the LORD, and made them commit a great sin. 22 For the children of Israel walked in all the sins of Jeroboam which he did; they did not depart from them, 23 until the LORD removed Israel out of His sight, as He had said by all His servants the prophets. So Israel was carried away from their own land to Assyria, as it is to this day.*

Israel rebelled against both the house of David and the God of their forefathers when they chose to follow Jeroboam instead of Solomon's son Rehoboam. Jeroboam was the one who built the golden calves for Israel to worship. He wanted to prevent his subjects from wanting to go up to Jerusalem to worship God and, eventually, desiring to reunite with Judah. Jeroboam was successful in making the split permanent. Even one hundred thirty years after Israel fell to Assyria, when Judah also went into captivity, Jeremiah refers to the two nations separately.

Jeremiah 30:3 NKJV 3 'For behold, the days are coming,' says the LORD, 'that I will bring back from captivity My people Israel and Judah,' says the LORD. 'And I will cause them to return to the land that I gave to their fathers, and they shall possess it.'"

Jeremiah was prophesying about the eventual return of both Israel and Judah to the Promised Land. There will come a time when the call on Mt. Ephraim is a call to go up to Jerusalem to worship!

Jeremiah 31:6 NKJV 6 For there shall be a day When the watchmen will cry on Mount Ephraim, 'Arise, and let us go up to Zion, To the LORD our God.'"

This is in sharp contrast to the call to worship that Jereboam issued. Jeroboam built the golden calves for Israel to worship, setting one up in Bethel in the tribal lands of Ephraim and one in Dan. Jeroboam commanded his subjects to come to worship the calves in Bethel and Dan!

1 Kings 12:28-29 NKJV 28 Therefore the king asked advice, made two calves of gold, and said to the people, "It is too much for you to go up to Jerusalem. Here are your gods, O Israel, which brought you up from the land of Egypt!" 29 And he set up one in Bethel, and the other he put in Dan.

When the call comes to worship in Jerusalem, Ephraim will go up with weeping and mourning.

Jeremiah 31:9 NKJV 9 They shall come with weeping,
And with supplications I will lead them. I will cause
them to walk by the rivers of waters, In a straight way
in which they shall not stumble; For I am a Father to
Israel, And Ephraim is My firstborn.

Ephraim will come with true repentance and God will hear
His voice.

Jeremiah 31:18-19 NKJV 18 "I have surely heard
Ephraim bemoaning himself: 'You have chastised me,
and I was chastised, Like an untrained bull; Restore
me, and I will return, For You are the LORD my God.
19 Surely, after my turning, I repented; And after I was
instructed, I struck myself on the thigh; I was ashamed,
yes, even humiliated, Because I bore the reproach of
my youth.'

Zechariah says that God will have mercy on both the house
of Judah and Joseph. Ephraim is, of course, Joseph's son.
Both the tribes of Ephraim and Manasseh, Joseph's two sons,
were part of the northern kingdom of Israel.

Zechariah 10:6-7 NKJV 6 "I will strengthen the house
of Judah, And I will save the house of Joseph. I will
bring them back, Because I have mercy on them. They
shall be as though I had not cast them aside; For I am
the LORD their God, And I will hear them. 7 Those of
Ephraim shall be like a mighty man, And their heart
shall rejoice as if with wine. Yes, their children shall

see it and be glad; Their heart shall rejoice in the LORD.

The word for mercy in this passage is "racham." Racham is related to the word rechem which is the word for womb. God will take both Judah and Ephraim once again as His beloved children. The word choice for the house of Judah and the house of Joseph is interesting. Judah is strengthened, while Joseph is saved. The Hebrew word for "strengthen' in this passage is the word "gabar", #1396 meaning to be strong or mighty. The word for save is "yasha", #3467, which is the root word of Yeshua's name "Salvation." It seems as if Judah will already be saved and will, at this point, just need God's strength. But Joseph first needs salvation; afterwards Ephraim shall also be like a mighty man. I can't help but think of another son of Joseph whom God called a" mighty man of valor". God called Gideon, from the tribe of Joseph's son Manasseh, a "mighty man of valor" when He called Gideon to deliver Israel from the hand of the Midianites.

Judges 6:12 NKJV 12 And the Angel of the LORD appeared to him, and said to him, "The LORD is with you, you mighty man of valor!"

The battle that Gideon fights with his three hundred men armed with lanterns and shofarim was fought in the valley of Megiddo and foreshadows the battle that Yeshua will fight at Har-Megiddo, the mountains of Megiddo.

Ezekiel writes about the reunification of Judah and Ephraim. But before we examine this passage, we need to examine the pattern of unity that we have come across throughout this book. In every situation, unity has been disrupted by conflict, then God acts to restore that unity and the power of God is released. Ezekiel 37:21-28 and Ezekiel 39:25-29 are very similar passages. They proclaim that God will bring back the children of Israel or Jacob from the nations where they have been scattered. He will sanctify them and dwell with them.

In the first passage, we read that David will be their king and that God restores the covenant of peace with them. In the other passage, we read that God will have poured out His Spirit on them. In between these two passages is the account of the Gog-Magog War. These two passages are about the same event with the Ezekiel 39 passage summarizing the events described in Ezekiel 37 that lead up to the Gog-Magog War.

Ezekiel describes Judah and Ephraim as two sticks being joined together in one hand.

Ezekiel 37:15-16 NKJV 15 Again the word of the LORD came to me, saying, 16 "As for you, son of man, take a stick for yourself and write on it: 'For Judah and for the children of Israel, his companions.' Then take another stick and write on it, 'For Joseph, the stick of Ephraim, and for all the house of Israel, his companions.'

The division between the people is interesting. Judah is grouped with the children of Israel, his companions, and Ephraim is grouped with the house of Israel, his companions. What is the difference between the children of Israel and the house of Israel? To answer this question, we ask another question: "Who stayed with Rehoboam of the house of Judah, and who went with Jereboam of the house of Ephraim?" They were mostly, but not entirely separated by tribe. The entire tribe of Judah and Benjamin stayed with Rehoboam, but others joined them as well.

Jeroboam rejected the Levites as priests choosing to select his own priests from whomever he chose. So, the Levites all went to Judah.

2 Chronicles 11:14 NKJV 14 For the Levites left their common-lands and their possessions and came to Judah and Jerusalem, for Jeroboam and his sons had rejected them from serving as priests to the LORD.

Those who were faithful to God also left Jeroboam's kingdom when he built the golden calves and presented them to the people as their gods.

2 Chronicles 11:15-16 NKJV 15 Then he appointed for himself priests for the high places, for the demons, and the calf idols which he had made. 16 And after the Levites left, those from all the tribes of Israel, such as set their heart to seek the LORD God of Israel, came to

Jerusalem to sacrifice to the LORD God of their fathers.

It is interesting that the scriptures say that the addition of the Levites and the faithful served to strengthen Judah for three years because Rehoboam walked with the LORD for these three years!

2 Chronicles 11:17 NKJV 17 So they strengthened the kingdom of Judah, and made Rehoboam the son of Solomon strong for three years, because they walked in the way of David and Solomon for three years.

Overall, the people who stayed with Rehoboam and Judah were those who were faithful to God and the house of David. These are the ones Ezekiel calls the children of Israel.

Those who stayed with Jeroboam participated in Jeroboam's sin. Over and over again, at the coronation of every king of Israel, we read that they "walked in the way of Jeroboam and in his sin which he had committed to make Israel sin." These are the ones called the house of Israel, the companions of Ephraim. Ephraim and the house of Israel consisted only of the physical descendants of Jacob. The children of Israel, the companions of Judah, consisted of not only the physical descendants of Jacob, but of those who were faithful to God.

Ezekiel was told to take the two sticks and join them together as one.

Ezekiel 37:17 (J. P. Green Interlinear Bible) And draw them one to one for yourself, into one stick. And they shall become for oneness in your hand.

This short sentence uses the word one, or in Hebrew, "echad" four times! One of the uses is in an unusual form, "echadim," a dual plural that Green translates as "oneness."[3] Judah and Ephraim are to be one! They will never be divided again!

Ezekiel 37:22 NKJV 22 "and I will make them one nation in the land, on the mountains of Israel; and one king shall be king over them all; they shall no longer be two nations, nor shall they ever be divided into two kingdoms again.

God goes on to state that they will never again go after false gods, but instead they will be His people!

Ezekiel 37:23 NKJV 23 "They shall not defile themselves anymore with their idols, nor with their detestable things, nor with any of their transgressions; but I will deliver them from all their dwelling places in which they have sinned, and will cleanse them. Then they shall be My people, and I will be their God.

---

[3] The Interlinear Bible, Volume III; Jay P Green, Sr; Hendrikson Publishers; 1985; Page 1997.

Then we come to the story of Gog who invades Israel when its inhabitants are dwelling in safety.

Ezekiel 38:8 NKJV 8 "After many days you will be visited. In the latter years you will come into the land of those brought back from the sword and gathered from many people on the mountains of Israel, which had long been desolate; they were brought out of the nations, and now all of them dwell safely.

We know the story, when Gog invades Israel, God acts decisively to destroy the armies of Gog! Like with the Midianites at the time of Gideon, they will turn on each other!

Ezekiel 38:21-23 NKJV 21 "I will call for a sword against Gog throughout all My mountains," says the Lord GOD. "Every man's sword will be against his brother. 22 "And I will bring him to judgment with pestilence and bloodshed; I will rain down on him, on his troops, and on the many peoples who are with him, flooding rain, great hailstones, fire, and brimstone. 23 "Thus I will magnify Myself and sanctify Myself, and I will be known in the eyes of many nations. Then they shall know that I am the LORD."'

The defeat of the armies of Gog will be undeniably the act of God! There will be no way the defeat can be attributed to any act of man. This is the power of God that will be released when Judah and Ephraim are joined back together as one people and one nation. The account of the Gog-Magog War ends with a reprise of the unity of Israel.

Ezekiel 39:27-29 NKJV 27 'When I have brought them back from the peoples and gathered them out of their enemies' lands, and I am hallowed in them in the sight of many nations, 28 'then they shall know that I am the LORD their God, who sent them into captivity among the nations, but also brought them back to their land, and left none of them captive any longer. 29 'And I will not hide My face from them anymore; for I shall have poured out My Spirit on the house of Israel,' says the Lord GOD."

David will be their king and God will have His dwelling place with them forever.

Ezekiel 37:27-28 NKJV 27 "My tabernacle also shall be with them; indeed I will be their God, and they shall be My people. 28 "The nations also will know that I, the LORD, sanctify Israel, when My sanctuary is in their midst forevermore."""

The word for "tabernacle" is mishkan, #7931 meaning dwelling place or residence. God will forever reside with Israel! This is the power of Echad!

We need to pray for strength and salvation for all of Israel. When Gog invades Israel, and he will do so, Ephraim and

Judah need to be one stick. They need to be one people united in love and worship of God.

Discussion Questions:

1. James, the brother of Yeshua, wrote an epistle to his brethren. Over and over in the book of James, he directly addresses his brethren. James 4:1-10 describes the source of enmity between brothers. What is that source and how is it combatted?

2. Proverbs 6:16-19 describes seven things that are an abomination to Him. One of them is to sow discord among brothers. How do all seven contribute to sowing discord?

One New Man

Ephesians 2:14-16 YLT 14 for he is our peace, who did make both one, and the middle wall of the enclosure did break down, 15 the enmity in his flesh, the law of the commands in ordinances having done away, that the two he might create in himself into one new man, making peace, 16 and might reconcile both in one body to God through the cross, having slain the enmity in it,

We have just learned about the power of God that will be released when the two sticks of Judah and Ephraim are once more joined together. Just like Ephraim and Judah have to come together reunited as one, so do the Jew and the Gentile. Ephraim and Judah need to be reunited under the banner of Israel; Jew and Gentile need to be reunited under the banner of the new man.

Earlier, we examined the power that the early believers in Yeshua had when they all came together in one accord. Thousands came to know and accept Yeshua as their savior. The power of healing was so evident that just being touched by Peter's shadow brought healing to the sick who lined the streets hoping he would walk by. This unity was rocked when the Gentiles began to believe in Yeshua as their savior as well. The friction between Gentile believers and mainstream Judaism increased until there was a complete split between the two. Although the covenants and the promises came through the Jewish people, the Gentile believers totally rejected anything resembling Judaism. The Jewish believers were caught in the middle! They had to choose between being rejected by their fellow Jews or by their fellow believers. This resulted in a body of believers consisting of Gentiles and Jews who had left their Jewish heritage behind. As we approach the return of Yeshua, there will once more be a vibrant body of Jewish believers in Messiah and Gentiles who embrace their Hebraic roots.

Paul's words in Ephesians about the one new man describe what this body of believers will look like. In order to understand the full meaning of Paul's letter, we need to look at the context under which he wrote it. The unity of the early church was disrupted by the inclusion of the Gentile believers. Factions within the growing body of Jewish believers refused to accept the Gentiles. The non-believers among the Jewish people wanted nothing to do with the Gentiles, especially the Jews in the diaspora. It was, in fact, the Jews from Asia who stirred up the riot which resulted in Paul's arrest in the temple.

Acts 21:27-30 NKJV 27 Now when the seven days were almost ended, the Jews from Asia, seeing him in the temple, stirred up the whole crowd and laid hands on him, 28 crying out, "Men of Israel, help! This is the man who teaches all men everywhere against the people, the law, and this place; and furthermore he also brought Greeks into the temple and has defiled this holy place." 2 (For they had previously seen Trophimus the Ephesian with him in the city, whom they supposed that Paul had brought into the temple.) 30 And all the city was disturbed; and the people ran together, seized Paul, and dragged him out of the temple; and immediately the doors were shut.

Paul was allowed to address the crowd before he was taken to the Roman garrison. Paul addressed the crowd in Hebrew, so they were willing to listen to him. He told them about Yeshua and His death and resurrection. And the crowd listened. Then, Paul told them that Yeshua had sent Paul to the Gentiles to share salvation with them as well. When Paul said that Yeshua told him to go to the Gentiles, the riot was renewed and Paul was taken away in chains.

Acts 22:21-22 NKJV 21 "Then He said to me, 'Depart, for I will send you far from here to the Gentiles.'" 22 And they listened to him until this word, and then they raised their voices and said, "Away with such a fellow from the earth, for he is not fit to live!"

As a Roman citizen, Paul was able to appeal the decision of his guilt or innocence to the current Caesar, Nero, so Paul was taken to Rome. He remained in Rome under house arrest until the death of Nero. When Nero died, and a new Caesar ascended the throne, everyone who was awaiting trial by Caesar Nero was immediately executed. This included the apostle Paul.

At the time that Paul wrote the letter to the Ephesian believers, he was at Rome awaiting trial. The Ephesian believers were very dear to Paul. He spent two years in Ephesus on his initial visit and used it as his headquarters in Asia. The Ephesian believers were mainly Gentiles because the Jews of the city as a group rejected the gospel.

Acts 19:8-10 NKJV 8 And he went into the synagogue and spoke boldly for three months, reasoning and persuading concerning the things of the kingdom of God. 9 But when some were hardened and did not believe, but spoke evil of the Way before the multitude, he departed from them and withdrew the disciples, reasoning daily in the school of Tyrannus. 10 And this continued for two years, so that all who dwelt in Asia heard the word of the Lord Jesus, both Jews and Greeks.

The Ephesians knew of all the difficulties Paul had with the Jewish leadership and the attempts to kill him.

Acts 20:17-21 NKJV 17 From Miletus he sent to Ephesus and called for the elders of the church. 18 And when they had come to him, he said to them: "You know, from the first day that I came to Asia, in what manner I always lived among you, 19 "serving the Lord with all humility, with many tears and trials which happened to me by the plotting of the Jews; 20 "how I kept back nothing that was helpful, but proclaimed it to you, and taught you publicly and from house to house, 21 "testifying to Jews, and also to Greeks, repentance toward God and faith toward our Lord Jesus Christ.

The believers in Ephesus were discouraged by Paul's imprisonment instigated by the non-believing Jews some of whom were probably from Ephesus. Paul encouraged them by reminding the Ephesian believers of the incredible gift of salvation that they had received through Yeshua. Paul concludes with these words:

Ephesians 3:13 NKJV 13 Therefore I ask that you do not lose heart at my tribulations for you, which is your glory.

The assembly of believers in Ephesus included both Jew and Gentile although they were mostly Gentiles. But both Jew and Gentile believers were opposed by the non-believing

Jews in the city. It is from this background and in this context that Paul writes the letter to all the believers in Ephesus.

Ephesians 1:1-2 NKJV 1 Paul, an apostle of Jesus Christ by the will of God, To the saints who are in Ephesus, and faithful in Christ Jesus: 2 Grace to you and peace from God our Father and the Lord Jesus Christ.

Paul wrote that Yeshua revealed that the mystery of His will was the unity of the body of Christ.

Ephesians 1:9-10 NKJV 9 having made known to us the mystery of His will, according to His good pleasure which He purposed in Himself, 10 that in the dispensation of the fullness of the times He might gather together in one all things in Christ, both which are in heaven and which are on earth--in Him.

Paul wrote that the gathering together in one was a future event. All things would be gathered at the proper time! The J. P. Green literal version of this passage reads a little differently giving us a different perspective. It reads:

Ephesians 1:9-10 (JPGreen Literal Version) 9 making known to us the mystery of His will, according to His good pleasure which He purposed in Himself, 10 for the administration of the fullness of time; to head up all things in Christ, both the things in heaven and the things on earth, in Him.

This passage focuses on Christ as the head which leads into Christ being the head over the body. The idea is still that of being one in Christ. Chapter 1 concludes with Paul stating that Yeshua is the head of the church.

Ephesians 1:22-23 NKJV 22 And He put all things under His feet, and gave Him to be head over all things to the church, 23 which is His body, the fullness of Him who fills all in all.

So, Paul is telling us that we will be gathered together in one body with Christ as the head. Paul addressed this same theme in his letters to the Corinthians and the Colossians. To the Colossians, he wrote that Yeshua was the head of the body.

Colossians 1:18 NKJV 18 And He is the head of the body, the church, who is the beginning, the firstborn from the dead, that in all things He may have the preeminence

To the Corinthians, Paul wrote that we are all believers and, together, we make up the body of Christ.

1 Corinthians 12:12-14 NKJV 12 For as the body is one and has many members, but all the members of that one body, being many, are one body, so also is Christ. 13 For by one Spirit we were all baptized into one body--whether Jews or Greeks, whether slaves or free--and have all been made to drink into one Spirit. 14 For in fact the body is not one member but many.

Paul continues in this discourse to the Corinthians to discuss the absurdity of the eye saying it has no need for the hand, or for the head to say it has no need of the feet. In order for the body to operate properly, it must work together. There cannot be hostility or pride between its members.

1 Corinthians 12:24b-25 NKJV 24b But God composed the body, having given greater honor to that part which lacks it, 25 that there should be no schism in the body, but that the members should have the same care for one another.

This is a common theme among Paul's letters. In chapter 12 of Romans, Paul, also, includes the idea that we are one body with Yeshua as its head. So, as we move into Ephesians chapter 2 and the concept of "One new man," we take with us the image of a man with many parts with Yeshua as the head. We, also, take with us the knowledge that there was enmity between Jew and Gentile in the Ephesian church.

Paul explains that we are able to have peace within the body, in this context between Jew and Gentile, because Yeshua, our head, is our peace.

Ephesians 2:14-16 YLT 14 for he is our peace, who did make both one, and the middle wall of the enclosure did break down, 15 the enmity in his flesh, the law of the commands in ordinances having done away, that the two he might create in himself into one new man, making peace, 16 and might reconcile both in one body to God through the cross, having slain the enmity in it,

In this context, to read that Yeshua broke down the enmity in his flesh, we have an "ah ha!" moment. This is the enmity between the hand and foot, the eye and the hand, between the body parts. He is the head; He is the preeminent body part; He is the ultimate authority over all things in the body. Further, this one new man is not separate from Yeshua; it is Yeshua! The words read, "That the two he might create **in himself** into one new man."

Have you ever been asked what the "One new man" is? I have, and the answer everyone seems to be looking for is not how we see the unification of Jew and Gentile. They are looking for the answer to the question of "Do the Gentiles have to follow Torah?" The real answer to what is the "One new man," is Yeshua is the "One new man!" We are included in the one new man through Him, and with Him. It doesn't matter if we are Jew or Gentile; we are one body with Yeshua as the head.

The original man, Adam, brought death to all men through disobedience. Yeshua, through His obedience, brought the gift of life.

Romans 5:17-18 NKJV 17 For if by the one man's offense death reigned through the one, much more those who receive abundance of grace and of the gift of righteousness will reign in life through the One, Jesus Christ. 18 Therefore, as through one man's offense judgment came to all men, resulting in condemnation, even so through one Man's righteous act the free gift came to all men, resulting in justification of life.

All of us, Jew or Gentile can receive the free gift of life and, as a result, become part of the body of Messiah. There is no longer a barrier between Jew and Gentile. Paul said in Ephesians 2:14 that the middle wall of the enclosure was broken down. The middle wall of the enclosure is the wall set up in the temple that separates the court of the Gentiles from the rest of the temple which contains the brazen altar of offering and the temple itself. The NKJV Study Bible explains in a comment on Ephesians 2:14:[4]

"The middle wall of separation between Jews and Gentiles was vividly portrayed by an actual partition in the temple area, with a sign warning that any Gentile going beyond the Court of the Gentiles would receive swift and sudden death."

---

[4] *The NKJV Study Bible* ; copyright ©1997, 2007 by Thomas Nelson, Inc.; p.1862.

Gentiles did not have access to the brazen altar to bring an offering and approach God. They had to get a Jewish man to bring the offering for them! Moses explained that anyone who wished to draw near to God had to bring an offering.

Leviticus 1:2 KJV 2 Speak unto the children of Israel, and say unto them, If any man of you bring an offering unto the LORD, ye shall bring your offering of the cattle, even of the herd, and of the flock.

The Hebrew word for "bring" is qarab, #7126 meaning to approach. The Hebrew word for "offering" is qorban, #7133 meaning something brought near. The offering—that which is brought near to God—allows a person to draw near to God.

Paul explained that the Gentiles who were once far away have now been brought near.

Ephesians 2:13 NKJV 13 But now in Christ Jesus you who once were far off have been brought near by the blood of Christ.

There is no longer a spiritual separation between Jew and Gentile. Yeshua is our offering that brings us near to God! In Paul's day, the physical wall of separation still existed. When Paul came up to Jerusalem amid rumors that he was teaching that the Torah was done away with, the leaders of the believers instructed Paul on how to show that the rumors were not true.

Acts 21:23-24 NKJV 23 "Therefore do what we tell you: We have four men who have taken a vow. 24 "Take them and be purified with them, and pay their expenses so that they may shave their heads, and that all may know that those things of which they were informed concerning you are nothing, but that you yourself also walk orderly and keep the law.

While in the temple on the seventh day of his purification, Paul was accused of bringing a Greek into the temple.

Acts 21:27-29 NKJV 27 Now when the seven days were almost ended, the Jews from Asia, seeing him in the temple, stirred up the whole crowd and laid hands on him, 28 crying out, "Men of Israel, help! This is the man who teaches all men everywhere against the people, the law, and this place; and furthermore he also brought Greeks into the temple and has defiled this holy place." 29 (For they had previously seen Trophimus the Ephesian with him in the city, whom they supposed that Paul had brought into the temple.)

Paul did not bring Trophimus into the temple. The actual physical wall of the enclosure was still in place. It is the spiritual wall of separation that Paul said has been done away with. Metaphorically, the barrier keeping Gentiles away from God is gone. Trophimus could not go into the temple. He could not personally bring an offering to the physical altar in the temple. However, there was no barrier preventing him from spiritually entering the heavenly temple because Yeshua brought the offering that allowed him to draw near to God!

As we continue examining Paul's statement in Ephesians 2, verse 15 says that "the enmity in his flesh, the law of the commands in ordinances having done away." The enmity between Jew and Gentile has been done away with as have "the law of the commands in ordinances." What is "the law of the commands in ordinances?" We have already seen that Paul continued to follow the Torah, so the Torah has not been done away with. The context is something that separates Jew and Gentile.

In addition to the wall of the enclosure in the temple, there were partitions in the synagogues separating the Gentile God-fearers from the Jews. These partitions are representative of all the man-made laws that kept Jews and Gentiles apart. These laws of separation forbade any Jewish person from eating with a Gentile or even entering into their homes! John refers to the restriction of entering the home of a Gentile in John 18:28:

John 18:28 NKJV 28 Then they led Jesus from Caiaphas to the Praetorium, and it was early morning. But they themselves did not go into the Praetorium, lest they should be defiled, but that they might eat the Passover.

Going into the Praetorium, a place where Gentiles gathered, would have made them ritually unclean until the next day according to the Jewish laws instituted by the ruling body. There is nothing in the scriptures that say entering a Gentile home or business would make a person unclean. However, the reasoning goes that there would be a greater chance of accidentally becoming unclean, therefore it would be better not to even enter the home or business to avoid the possibility altogether. And so, the restriction was made law.

Luke refers to this restriction in Acts 11 when he relates the reaction of the unbelievers to Peter entering the home of the Gentile Cornelius and eating with him.

Acts 11:2-3 NKJV 2 And when Peter came up to Jerusalem, those of the circumcision contended with him, 3 saying, "You went in to uncircumcised men and ate with them!"

The Pharisees also refer to these additional man-made laws when questioning the practices of Yeshua's disciples in Matthew.

Matthew 15:2 NKJV 2 "Why do Your disciples transgress the tradition of the elders? For they do not wash their hands when they eat bread."

These additional "laws" were called a barrier or hedge around the Torah. The Greek word used in the Talmud to describe this barrier around the Torah is the same Greek word used for "wall of the enclosure" in the Ephesians passage. Paul, as a Pharisee, was familiar with this practice and this phrase.

The Zondervan NIV Study Bible, in a commentary on Ephesians 2:15, says:

> "Since Matthew 5:17 and Romans 3:31 teach that God's moral standard expressed in the OT law is not changed by the coming of Christ, what is abolished here is probably the effect of the specific "commandments and regulations" in separating Jews from Gentiles, whose nonobservance of the Jewish law renders them ritually unclean."[5]

So, "the law of the commands in ordinances" is an explanation for "the wall of the enclosure." Verse 15 is a repeat of verse 14 in slightly different terms. This is a common "Hebraic" construct! In fact, verse 16 is also parallel to verse 14! The enmity in the body is an explanation for the wall of the enclosure. The words that have parallel meaning in each verse are highlighted in bold type below, and then broken down into the chart that follows.

14: for he is our **peace**, who did make both **one**, and the **middle wall of the enclosure** did **break down**,

---

[5] Zondervan NIV Study Bible copyright ©1985, 1995, 2002, 2008 by Zondervan; p.1827.

15: the **enmity in his flesh, the law of the commands in ordinances** having **done away**, that the two he might create in himself into **one new man**, making **peace**,
16: and might **reconcile** both in **one body** to God **through the cross**, having **slain the enmity in it**,

14	Peace	One	Middle wall of enclosure	Break down
15	Peace	One new man	Enmity in his flesh Law of commands in ordinances	Done away
16	Reconcile through the cross	One body	the enmity	Slain

Paul repeated himself in these verses saying the same things three times! This indicates the importance of this concept. We are one body whose head is Christ. We are together with Christ one new man! Paul's message is a message of reconciliation and inclusion. The Gentiles are included in salvation and in the one new man.

Verses 1 through 16 tell us that Yeshua is our peace; He makes us one new man in His body. The middle wall of the enclosure representing the enmity instituted by man-made ordinances is broken down, done away with, slain in His flesh!

Paul is reminding the largely Gentile Ephesians, who were irate that Paul was in chains because of the false accusations of some of the Jews, that Yeshua did away with the enmity between Jew and Gentile. They are to put away their bad feelings and love each other.

Ephesians 4:1-3 NKJV 1 I, therefore, the prisoner of the Lord, beseech you to walk worthy of the calling with which you were called, 2 with all lowliness and gentleness, with longsuffering, bearing with one another in love, 3 endeavoring to keep the unity of the Spirit in the bond of peace.

They were not just supposed to love their fellow Gentile believers; they were to love their Jewish brethren as well! Paul makes that clear as he goes on to emphasize they are one!

Ephesians 4:4-6 NKJV 4 There is one body and one Spirit, just as you were called in one hope of your calling; 5 one Lord, one faith, one baptism; 6 one God and Father of all, who is above all, and through all, and in you all.

Paul goes on to talk about the roles and gifts given to various members of the body. He explains that the purpose of the roles and gifts is to help the body achieve unity.

Ephesians 4:11-13 NKJV 11 And He Himself gave some to be apostles, some prophets, some evangelists, and some pastors and teachers, 12 for the equipping of the saints for the work of ministry, for the edifying of the body of Christ, 13 till we all come to the unity of

119

the faith and of the knowledge of the Son of God, to a perfect man, to the measure of the stature of the fullness of Christ;

The goal of building up the body in one new man is the establishment of the body of Messiah as a temple!

Ephesians 2:19-21 NKJV 19 Now, therefore, you are no longer strangers and foreigners, but fellow citizens with the saints and members of the household of God, 20 having been built on the foundation of the apostles and prophets, Jesus Christ Himself being the chief cornerstone, 21 in whom the whole building, being joined together, grows into a holy temple in the Lord,

So, what happens when the body acts as one? What happens when we walk together as "One new man?" Paul describes what will happen when the whole body comes together as one. The whole body, Jew and Gentile, will be cleansed and sanctified through the word of God!

Ephesians 5:25-27 KJV 25 Husbands, love your wives, even as Christ also loved the church, and gave himself for it; 26 That he might sanctify and cleanse it with the washing of water by the word, 27 That he might present it to himself a glorious church, not having spot, or wrinkle, or any such thing; but that it should be holy and without blemish.

The assembly will be ready to be presented to Yeshua as a fitting bride without blemish! Yeshua has been loving His church and will continue to love it until He has completed the work of transforming us into one body under His headship.

Paul has given us a mixture of metaphors. In chapter 2, it was the metaphor of the "One new man" and the temple of God. In chapter 5, it is the metaphor of the bride. The apostle John continues the metaphor of the bride in the Book of the Revelation of Jesus Christ.

Revelation 19:6-8 NKJV 6 And I heard, as it were, the voice of a great multitude, as the sound of many waters and as the sound of mighty thunderings, saying, "Alleluia! For the Lord God Omnipotent reigns! 7 "Let us be glad and rejoice and give Him glory, for the marriage of the Lamb has come, and His wife has made herself ready." 8 And to her it was granted to be arrayed in fine linen, clean and bright, for the fine linen is the righteous acts of the saints.

This event that John describes occurs after the fall of Babylon and the coronation of Yeshua as king. The unity of the body in Yeshua releases the power and authority that brings about the destruction of Babylon and the Antichrist.

Revelation 19:1-2 NKJV 1 After these things I heard a loud voice of a great multitude in heaven, saying, "Alleluia! Salvation and glory and honor and power belong to the Lord our God! 2 "For true and righteous are His judgments, because He has judged the great harlot who corrupted the earth with her fornication; and He has avenged on her the blood of His servants shed by her."

So, as we get closer to the time when Yeshua will return, let us endeavor to be one body; Jew with Jew, Gentile with Gentile, Jew with Gentile. Let us practice walking as Yeshua walked and allowing the Holy Spirit to work in us both individually and corporately. Paul summarizes this nicely:

Ephesians 5:17-21 NKJV 17 Therefore do not be unwise, but understand what the will of the Lord is. 18 And do not be drunk with wine, in which is dissipation; but be filled with the Spirit, 19 speaking to one another in psalms and hymns and spiritual songs, singing and making melody in your heart to the Lord, 20 giving thanks always for all things to God the Father in the name of our Lord Jesus Christ, 21 submitting to one another in the fear of God.

Discussion Questions:

1. What are the characteristics that Paul describes as being of the "old man" and the "new man" in Colossians 3:4-17?

2. The New Jerusalem that comes out of heaven is described as the bride in Revelation 21:9-27. What characteristics of the New Jerusalem emphasize the importance of unity of heart between brothers and unity of heart toward God?

Summary

As Yeshua was praying in the Garden of Gethsemane in the night-hours before His arrest and crucifixion, He poured out His heart to His Father God. In that prayer, Yeshua prays for all of His followers both those alive at that time and those who would follow Him throughout the ages. His prayer is for unity.

John 17:20-21 NKJV 20 "I do not pray for these alone, but also for those who will believe in Me through their word; 21 "that they all may be one, as You, Father, are in Me, and I in You; that they also may be one in Us, that the world may believe that You sent Me.

Yeshua doesn't pray for unity just for the sake of unity; He prays for unity with the Father so that the entire world may believe that Yeshua is the Sent One of God! Yeshua said that God sent Him into the world so that the world would have the opportunity for eternal life.

John 3:16-17 NKJV 16 "For God so loved the world that He gave His only begotten Son, that whoever believes in Him should not perish but have everlasting life. 17 "For God did not send His Son into the world to condemn the world, but that the world through Him might be saved.

If you have not already accepted Yeshua as your gateway to fellowship with God the Father, you can have that today just by believing in your heart and confessing with your mouth that Yeshua is the Son of God sent to die in your place. If you have made that decision, today, to accept Yeshua as your Messiah, let us know by contacting us through our website www.moedministries.com.

Our prayer for the body of believers is that God would make us all one in Yeshua, one in the Father, and one in each other.

Shalom and be blessed!

Made in the USA
Lexington, KY
28 September 2017